The Guilded Pen

Third Edition 2014

An anthology of the San Diego Writers/Editors Guild

Marcia Buompensiero, Editor
Simone Arias, Poetry Editor

San Diego
Writers Editors
Since 1979
Guild

The Guilded Pen, Third Edition

The Guilded Pen, Third Edition is a publication of the
San Diego Writers/Editors Guild
P.O. Box 881931, San Diego, CA 92168-1931
www.sdwritersguild.org

The Guilded Pen, Third Edition was printed by CreateSpace,
an Amazon.com Company, and is available in hard cover or e-book
format at: www.CreateSpace.com. Hard cover copies may also be
ordered from our website: www.sdwritersguild.org..

Marcia Buompensiero, Editor; Simone Arias, Poetry Editor

"First Noel" by Alan Russell. Excerpt from *St. Nick*, published in the United
States by Amazon Publishing, 2013 (Thomas & Mercer imprint, 2013).
Used with permission of Amazon Publishing, www.apub.com, all rights
reserved. Reprinted by permission of the author.

"The Gambler" by Carolyn Jaynes. Originally published in *Sprinkles From Heaven*
(Passion & Faith Press, 2014). Reprinted by permission of the author.

"The Meeting" by Lisa Hunt. Originally published in *One Salute Too Many*
(CreateSpace Independent Publishing Platform, 2013). Reprinted by permission
of the author.

"Words and Music" by John Cain. Originally published in *Life's A Good Gig*
(Enertia/All World Music, 2007). Reprinted by permission of the author.

"A Family's Journey" by Charlotte E. Thompson, M.D. Originally published in
Letters Home (Trafford Publishing, 2005). Reprinted by permission of the author.

Cover Art – Marcia Buompensiero
Price: $15.00

ISBN-10: 0692264639
ISBN-13: 978-0692264638

The Guilded Pen

Third Edition, 2014

TABLE OF CONTENTS

TABLE OF CONTENTS (CONT'D)

ACKNOWLEDGEMENTS

The Guilded Pen would not have been possible without our contributors. We are grateful to you for sharing your work for publication in *The Guilded Pen, Third Edition*.

Additionally, we are grateful for the support and dedication of our review panel, the SDW/EG Board of Directors: Gered Beeby, Bob Doublebower, Harry Huntsman, Ruth Leyse-Wallace, Rick Peterson and Ellen Shaw Tufts.

A very special note of appreciation to Dave Feldman, our untiring copyeditor.

Message from the President

Harry W. Huntsman

After millions of years of human evolution, writing was invented to communicate with others beyond the range of the human voice and to overcome the limitations of the oral message bearer.

Literacy is still in its adolescence when compared to other human developments. The mission of the San Diego Writers/ Editors Guild is to enhance the utility and pleasure of literacy, both writing and reading. Publication of the Guild's anthology is a giant step toward this goal.

Many skilled conversationalists and storytellers lack the confidence and patience needed to learn the craft of writing. Members of the Guild who write their stories, memoirs, poems, etc., have paid the price, made the effort, and endured the loneliness to become writers.

As a pastoral counselor, I sometimes ask counselees to read and discuss with me books or articles appropriate to their problems or needs. I have added some works from the Guild's anthologies to my list of writings that teach and heal.

Working with the members of the Guild's board of directors this year has increased my passion to write.

Introduction

Marcia Buompensiero

Editor

Writers can't not write.

Goaded by dreams and thoughts, writers write because they'll simply burst if they don't.

They have these urges to get it all out—from A to Z—from soup to nuts. They tackle those germs of thought, feeding and weeding and coaxing them to grow, perchance to blossom into something worthwhile. Something beautiful. Something to challenge or inspire.

This year's anthology, a compilation of the various forms of the art, is all that—and more. Our contributors stepped up their game. As a result, we bring you a bouquet of literary talent represented in memoir, poetry, essay and creative writing.

Whether fact or fiction from seasoned and multi-published veterans, or authors making their publishing debut, the contributors have drawn from their own life experiences or the thoughts bumping around in their heads. They spun yarns. They told tales. They opened doors to the imagination—conjuring, questioning, and stirring up. They glimpsed other worlds and they've brought them to you.

They did what they must. They wrote.

Introduction

Simone Arias

Poetry Editor

Thank you to the muses of poetry who tickle and throttle. Your lofty to elemental snapshots of life entice us to ponder the infinite in the moment by amplifying the human spirit. We celebrate your inspiration. May future editions perpetuate those captured experiences for everyone — from creative curious children to seasoned citizens.

The Guilded Pen, Third Edition

There is no greater agony than bearing an untold story inside you.

Maya Angelou

How I Write

Richard Lederer

Ernest Hemingway's first rule for writers was to apply the seat of the pants to the seat of the chair. But not all authors are able to survive with such a simple approach.

Emile Zola pulled the shades and composed by artificial light. Francis Bacon, we are told, knelt each day before creating his greatest works. Martin Luther could not write unless his dog was lying at his feet, while Ben Jonson needed to hear his cat purring.

Marcel Proust sealed out the world by lining the walls of his study with cork. Gertrude Stein and Raymond Carver wrote in their cars, while Edmond Rostand preferred to write in his bathtub. Emily Dickinson hardly ever left her home and garden. Wallace Stevens composed poetry while walking to and from work each day at a Hartford insurance company. Alexander Pope and Jean Racine could not write without first declaiming at the top of their voices. Jack Kerouac began each night of writing by kneeling in prayer and composing by candlelight. Dan Brown rises to write at 4 a.m. seven days a week. As an antidote to the dreaded writer's block, he hangs upside down like a bat until the creative juices begin flowing. Friedrich Schiller started each of his writing sessions by opening the drawer of his desk and breathing in the fumes of the rotten apples he had stashed there.

Some writers have donned and doffed gay apparel. Early in his career, John Cheever wore a business suit as he traveled from his apartment to a room in his basement. Then he hung the suit on a hanger and wrote in his underwear. Jessamyn West wrote in bed without getting dressed, as, from time to time, did Eudora Welty, Edith Wharton, Mark Twain, and Truman Capote. John McPhee worked in his bathrobe and tied its sash to the arms of his chair to keep from even thinking about deserting his writing room.

For stimulation, Honoré de Balzac wrote in a monk's costume and drank at least twenty cups of coffee a day, eventually dying of caffeine poisoning. As his vision failed, James Joyce took to wearing a milkman's uniform when he wrote, believing that its whiteness caught the sunlight and reflected it onto his pages. Victor Hugo went to the opposite lengths to ensure his daily output of words on paper. He gave all his clothes to his servant with orders that they be returned only after he had finished his day's quota.

Compared to such strategies, my daily writing regimen is drearily normal. Perhaps that's because I'm a nonfictionalist — a hunter-gatherer of language who records the sounds that escape from the holes in people's faces, leak from their pens, and luminesce up on their computer screens. I don't drink coffee. Rotten fruit doesn't inspire (literally "breathe into") me. My lifelong, heels-over-head love affair with language is my natural caffeine and fructose.

To be a writer, one must behave as writers behave. They write. And write. And write. The difference between a writer and a wannabe is that a writer is someone who can't not write, while a wannabe says, "One of these days when . . . then I'll. . . ." Unable not to write, I write almost every day.

A grocer doesn't wait to be inspired to go to the store, and a banker to go to the bank. I can't afford the luxury of waiting to be inspired before I go to work. Writing is my job, and it happens to be a job that almost nobody gives up on purpose. I love my job as a writer, so I write. Every day that I can.

Long ago, I discovered that I would never become the Great American Novelist. I stink at cobbling characters, dialogue, episode, and setting. You won't find much of that fictional stuff in my books, unless the story serves the ideas I am trying to communicate. A writer has to find out what kind of writer he or she is, and I somehow got born an English teacher with an ability to illuminate language and literature. In my work, ideas, not characters, are the heroes.

Jean-Jacques Rousseau wrote only in the early morning, Alain-Rene Lesage at midday, and Lord Byron at midnight. Early on, I also discovered that I am more lark than owl—more a morning person than a night person—and certainly not a bat, one who writes through the night. I usually hit the ground punning at around 7:30 a.m., and I'm banging away at the keyboard within an hour.

I write very little on paper, almost everything on my computer. Theodore Sturgeon once wrote, "Nine-tenths of everything is crap." The computer allows me to dump crap into the hard drive without the sense of permanence that handwriting or type on paper used to signify to me. I'm visual and shape my sentences and paragraphs most dexterously on a screen. The computer has not only trebled my output. It has made me a more joyful, liberated, and better writer.

Genetic and environmental roulette has allowed me to work in either a silent or a noisy environment. I'm a speaker as well as a writer, so phone calls and faxes and e-messages chirp and hum and buzz in my writing room, and I often have to answer them during those precious morning hours. That's all right with me. Fictionalists shut the world out. Fictionalists live with their imaginary characters, who get skittish and may flee a noisy room. As I cobble my essays, my readers are my companions, and they will usually stay with me in my writing space through outerworldly alarms and excursions.

Besides, the business of the writing business gives me the privilege of being a writer. In fact, I consider the writing only about half my job. Writers don't make a living writing books. They make a living selling books. After all, I do have to support my writing habit.

My whole life has been an effort to obliterate the distance between who I am and what I do. When you are heels over head in love with what you do, you never work a day. That's me: butt over teakettle in love with being a writer—a job that nobody who works it would give up on purpose.

The First Noel

Alan Russell

From *St. Nick*

November 28

It was Thanksgiving, but there was no aroma of roasting turkey wafting through the apartment. Nick Pappas had waited until noon to get out of bed. He hadn't slept in, though, and couldn't be sure he'd even slept at all. He had remained in bed because he lacked the impetus to get up, and was afraid of what he might do when he did.

Nick carried cereal and milk over to a warped vinyl dining table that he'd picked up at a garage sale for five bucks. The condiments were already on the table: salt, pepper, and sugar. And there was something else on the table, something metal, and dark, and ugly. He didn't look at the gun, not directly at least, but it was there.

The revolver had been next to the sugar for two weeks. It had started as a game, or that's what Nick tried to tell himself. One day he had taken the gun out of the closet; a few days later it was out of its holster. And then it went from the mantel, to the top of the refrigerator, to the counter, to the table. It kept getting closer to him. He could almost feel its heat.

He poured milk on his cereal, but didn't start eating right away. He wasn't really hungry. Maybe it wasn't cereal he wanted to eat.

No, it wasn't a game anymore. But then it never had been.

The gun was a revolver, a wheel gun—as in, spin the wheel. Young cops thought everything but semiautomatics were antiques— they wouldn't be caught dead with a wheel gun. Nick's was old, but it would do the job. The choice was in front of him: eat or be eaten.

Was that it? Was that the question? Nick wished he could care more, one way or the other, but he didn't. He was just tired. One final disappointment, he thought. But he wasn't ready to act, not quite yet. A small part of him was still holding out.

Maybe the department would reinstate him. Unlikely, he knew, but the Fat Lady hadn't sung yet. He could wait until the suits returned their verdict.

Was that it? Was that his best Clarence Darrow? He hadn't even brought up Teddy, or George, or Corinne. But there were reasons he hadn't. Teddy was an ex-wife, and George and Corinne were ex-kids, or close to it. They were probably all getting together today. Maybe some other man was going to be carving Teddy's bird.

Even if he was reinstated, Nick knew he'd always have the reputation as the departmental screwup. There, he felt something: a twinge of residual pride. He had messed up, done the wrong thing but for what he believed was the right reason. Maybe he could live with that. Maybe. But he'd just been skating on the job anyway, putting in the hours like other burnouts.

He looked at the revolver.

When he had started the ritual, he'd told himself there was no way he really wanted to die.

Liar.

Maybe he should take the bullets out of five of the chambers, and give it a spin. He could pull the trigger. He'd just do it once. And that way he wouldn't really be making the decision. Fate would.

Lying again. Nick knew he wouldn't stop at one attempt. And blaming fate was a cop-out.

He reached out with his hand. He still wasn't sure if he was reaching for the sugar or for the gun. His hand was halfway there when the phone rang.

Teddy, he thought. She had broken down and decided to invite him over for Thanksgiving dinner. But even as he reached for the phone he knew it wouldn't be Teddy. They had been divorced for almost five years now, and she had moved on with her life. She only talked with him when she had to, and that wasn't very often. Maybe it was Georgie or Corinne. The kids were a little more forgiving than Teddy, but not much.

As he picked up the receiver, Nick wished he had a cell phone with a display, or at least an answering machine. That way he could have screened who was calling. When he'd furnished the apartment a few years back he had done all his interior designing around a few garage sales. It was a shame no one had been selling an answering machine. By his own choice he didn't have a cell phone. He had lost his last cell phone just before everything hit the fan, and since then he'd seen no need to replace it. His home phone rang seldom enough.

"Got your bird in the oven yet, Nico?"

Forster. No one else called him Nico, at least not anymore. Forster had heard Nick's mom call him that. He and Forster had been young then, both of them working patrol. Of course, Forster had been smarter than Nick. He'd put in his twenty years and walked away with his pension and his health. Now he was well into his second career.

"Yeah," said Nick. "It's cooking right now."

"Don't lie to me, Nico. I'll bet you haven't used your oven once since you moved in."

"For your information, I've become quite the cook. I didn't buy some store stuffing. I filled my bird with a cornbread and chestnut stuffing."

"Something's full of it, but I don't think it's your bird."

"Being skeptical of others isn't a healthy way to live, Wally."

Forster hated being called Wally. He went by Walt, or even Walter, but never Wally.

He pretended not to notice. "Our bird is about to come out of the oven, Nico, and I'm not talking some fantasy turkey with chestnut and corn stuffing . . ."

"Cornbread."

"Whatever. This is a 20-pound bird. It's got a chest bigger

than a Las Vegas showgirl's. And for whatever reason, Maggie wants you to join us."

"I wish you'd told me before I made my stuffing."

Forster played along with the lie. "That's what refrigerators are for."

"I appreciate the offer. But I've got other plans."

"Maggie isn't the only one who wants you here. I was hoping we could talk business. I need you, Nico."

"For what?"

"Come over and we'll talk about it."

"I told you, I got plans."

"I need you starting tomorrow, Nick. That's when it all happens, you know. Christmas season."

Forster was the Director of Security for Plaza Center, one of San Diego's largest malls. "Doors open at five a.m. in some of the stores," he said. "My headache starts at five-oh-one."

"I'm no rent-a-cop."

"Don't need a rent-a-cop," Forster said. "I got enough of those. I need someone undercover. Two days ago we had a mugging. The victim is still in the I.C.U., and she wasn't the first. Two scumbags roughed her up. I need you on lookout while they're trying to scout other marks. We'll put you in a central location."

"I like the central location of my apartment."

"I'm asking for a favor. I got a lot of people breathing down my neck. Muggings don't help business and these guys are bad news."

Forster didn't give Nick a chance to decline the offer. "Besides, you owe me," he said.

"What do you mean I owe you?"

"You saved my life."

It had happened their second year on patrol. Forster had never seen the second gun. Nick had.

"That's right. So why do I owe you?"

"The Chinese say if you save someone's life, then you're responsible for them the rest of your life."

"You think I care what Confucius says? Here's your newsflash: I'm no Chinaman. I'm one hundred percent Greek, and we're talking the real thing, not the fratboy *I Eta Pi* kind of Greek."

"No, what you are is a cop. And when a cop's partner asks for help, you do whatever it takes."

"You haven't been my partner for years."

"What? There's a statute of limitations?"

Nick took a long breath. Forster sounded like he needed him for real. This wasn't like the charity minimum wage job he'd offered him when he had first been suspended from the force.

"A week," said Nick. "I'll do it for a week."

"Opa! I need you tomorrow morning, no later than seven, Nico. And you better wear your Kevlar vest."

"Why? Are the suspects armed?"

"Who said anything about the suspects? I'm talking about the shoppers. There's nothing quite as dangerous as the day-after-Thanksgiving sale."

Nick could hear the change in Forster's voice: He'd landed his fish. Now he was just playing with it.

"I can hardly wait."

"Do it, Nico. I don't even need to see it. Just do it so I can hear over the phone. That'll be good enough."

As empty as he was feeling, Nick still almost grinned. Anthony Quinn's *Zorba the Greek* had duped the whole world into thinking that Greeks everywhere loved to dance. Ever since seeing Zorba, Forster had been asking Nick to dance. That phony Quinn wasn't even Greek. He was Mexican.

"I don't dance, Wally."

"It's in your blood, Nico. You know it. You're denying yourself. That can't be healthy."

"I don't dance."

"Maybe not yet. But you're like an active volcano that's just waiting to erupt. And when it happens, I want to be there."

"Don't hold your breath."

"See you tomorrow, Nico."

Nick hung up the phone and went back to the table. He had this feeling the governor had called and given the condemned man another week to live. Nick wasn't sure whether he felt relieved or not.

He sat down and reached for the sugar.

The Find

Gered Beeby

"That's a mile away. How can you hear or see anything?"

Sylvia's hushed inquiry lingered in the night air. The Montana desert held any number of secrets. Their objective in the distance promised even more.

"Told you before, lady," Borden began quietly. "Gear like this, and my services, both come at a price. Let me handle the details."

Sylvia knew there would be issues. Her news agency assured her of that. She also knew the challenges of dealing with her long-time girlfriend, waiting several steps away and silent in the darkness.

"Look, Mr. Borden, you said you could get me and my associate into that place." She kept her voice low.

"And I also said I would get both you ladies back, safely. But whatever your friend's talents are, rock climbing is not one of them." Borden adjusted his night-vision scope. He peered from their slightly elevated vantage point. "Fairly open country from here. No moon, but we need to watch our cover. Also, you can drop the 'Mister.' Just call me Hal. And by the way, is that your friend's real name? Etheria?"

Sylvia nudged a bit closer. "Originally, she was Brenda. But her parents were, and still are, genuine flower children. They renamed her when she was young. Their early glimpses of her abilities convinced them."

"So she reads palms for a living? A psychic?" Borden also spoke in muted tones.

"More specifically, an Empath," Sylvia all but whispered. "She feels. Her powers are strongest with people. But she can function with animals and inanimate objects as well. And yes, she makes a living at it. Has a large ... a very large, and loyal following."

"Okay, okay, so far." Borden flicked a bug away from his scope. "And somehow, she's not able to work her magic from far away."

"Her skills, not magic, work best at close range. Yes, touching. But she has some capability at a distance. Hence, all the more reason for you to get us there. Soon." Sylvia adjusted her night-vision goggles.

Borden checked his latest-series communicator. "My contact assures me this is prime time. He's seen the Feds come and go, always by chopper. Probably from the air base at Great Falls. All this and they're still trying to keep a lid on it."

"This is a remote paleontology dig. The point becomes, why so secret?"

"Maybe we'll all learn." Borden rechecked his communicator, then stopped.

Silent as a shadow, Etheria had reached his side, then touched his arm.

"About eight meters ahead, under that bush, you may notice a sizable rattlesnake, Mr. Borden." Her voice trailed away, dissipated into the darkness.

Borden recalled again that first meeting, where Sylvia had introduced them. Tall, nearly as tall as he was, blond and thin, Etheria presented small, pixie-like features to the world. Her tone matched the image of one who sees much and appreciates even more.

He quickly aimed his goggles and exhaled. Coiled and still, the reptile seemed alert, but not yet alarmed. Borden slowly shook his head, "That's one big mother snake."

"You are correct, Mr. Borden." Etheria stepped one pace back. "She is gravid and seeks a safe place to berth her young. She also needs nourishment."

Sylvia joined the brief vigil with her glasses. "So, she's just making a living like the rest of us. I've known you too long, Etheria, to ask how you knew all that."

"Let's move on." Borden kept an eye on the bush and led his small party a safe distance around.

Lighting at the cordon was widely distributed, but subdued. Camouflage netting draped the entire area, about the size of a city block and positioned near a low hill. The woven-wire fencing was mostly clear, but draped in a few places.

Borden exchanged signals with his contact. The trio moved toward an entrance gate with its temporary kiosk. An armed man in military-style overalls approached from inside.

"Sam the Man, is this a good time?" Borden greeted his fellow conspirator.

The man unlocked the gate, rolled it open. "Yeah, but my relief's due in less than an hour. And sometimes he's early."

Quietly, Borden addressed the two women, "If you will stand over at that shed. I need a few words with Sam."

Sylvia took Etheria in tow. For some time her non-flash mini-camera had been collecting images. Neither woman said a word.

"Look, Hal, I gotta stay close to the gate. All security guys got chip implants done. Get too close to that entrance and some alarm goes off. Only reason I agreed was the pay was so good."

"How safe is it?"

"Fine; don't think anybody believes that radon gas story. But look, things may get really unsafe, if anybody gets caught." Sam looked around. "Remember, you promised me stuff. And you know the risk I'm taking."

"Once again, you say there are no cameras?"

"Not far as I can tell. My guess is they want no record of those bigwigs that come through. Overheard one of them, 'Profound implications.' So tell me what's profound about old bones and we'll both know."

"We'll be fast." Borden turned to join his charges, but got

restrained by Sam.

"And one more thing. Who's the Tall Tinkerbell?"

Borden delayed a moment. "Someone we need to listen to."

He rejoined the women. They reached the enclosed metal building near the hillside. Borden instinctively glanced about before entering.

The enclosure was complete with a metal roof, big enough to cover a one-story house. Interior curtains formed a light-restricting mouse maze. They reached the excavation.

Well-lit, the ancient remains lay partially exposed. Without a word, Sylvia clambered into the shallow pit. She began taking photos from multiple angles.

Etheria held back.

The find lay perfectly straight. Its bones were perfectly intact.

It was pygmy-sized, and its vacant eye sockets stared forever upward. Sharp teeth suggested a carnivorous diet. But the flattened jaw line indicated not a snout, but a face. One upper limb was mostly uncovered. Between the shoulder and elbow, encircling the bone and still lodged in rock, was metal.

"Copper alloy." Borden had joined Sylvia and pointed to the armlet. "And observe, shall I say, the hand. It has three digits, but with a clearly opposable thumb.

"And check out this." Borden traced his fingers along a straight edge of fossilized wood: primitive milled lumber. At a top corner near the skull, a reinforcing strap and nail-like fasteners were similarly fabricated. "Like a crib."

Sylvia stopped her photography. "With stereoscopic vision and functioning hands, clearly this creature could manipulate its environment. So this lonely little planet of ours supported Bronze Age intelligence tens of millions of years before we came along."

"One smart lizard." Borden cleared his throat. "This equals profound implications. But, obvious question, how come they aren't still here?"

Sylvia turned to her friend, who had yet to enter the pit. "Etheria, we would welcome your insight. Right now, please."

Throughout their investigation, Etheria had scarcely moved. Her inspection had been intense, yet silent. With measured precision, she descended, then stopped. "I'm frightened."

But with no further hesitation, Etheria approached the remains. Firmly at first, rigid, then trembling, Etheria's fingers enveloped the non-human cranium. Alternately pressing, then relieving, her fingertips worked to absorb unknown truth. Further and further into the ancient aura she probed until, facing the roof, she released her grip. Her body relaxed, then began to slump.

Both Sylvia and Borden stopped her fall.

"We must get her out of here!" Sylvia whispered sharply.

Quickly, Borden gathered Etheria into a fireman's carry. "I'm not waiting."

Eventually, they found a stopping point far enough away. Slumped over Borden's shoulders, Etheria had not stirred. He placed her on soft sand.

"Smelling salts are not part of my outfit." Borden wet a cloth from his canteen, but before he could use it Etheria stopped his hand.

"You are kind, Mr. Borden, both of you, but my processing is complete." She sat up, helped by Sylvia.

"I see you were overwhelmed, but what happened?" Sylvia found her cassette recorder.

Etheria forced composure. "Fleeting images, so many images and fears. Speculation clouds everything. Of a civilization grown to engulf the entire world. Of advances only now being realized in our own. Of unending conflict. Of devastation so complete that mass extinctions became commonplace." She paused.

"But eventually a shimmer of hope. And compassion. A limited few at first, then more, then eventually all perceived the truth. They must leave. And remove all traces of themselves, if possible. Then take their destructive natures with them. All to preserve the Eden they had nearly obliterated."

Sylvia exchanged somber looks with Borden. "Etheria, suppose all this is true. And these creatures had the means of evacuating … to somewhere. What then? Would they some day want their Eden back?"

No one could answer.

One by one, they lifted their eyes to the endless stars.

Cuckoo

Norma Posey

"In Italy, for thirty years under the Borgias, they had warfare, terror, murder, and bloodshed, but they produced Michelangelo, Leonardo da Vinci, and the Renaissance. In Switzerland, they had five hundred years of democracy and peace, and they produced the cuckoo clock." (From the movie "The Third Man," 1949.)

*

In a state of utter innocence and purity of heart, I stopped by to visit my good friend Pamela. I arrived to find her cleaning out a storage shed. The shed had seen better days and was slowly returning to the dust whence it had sprung. It had become something less than attractive, and Pamela, in a spirit of mercy, had threatened to hasten its demise.

"Whatcha doin?" asked I.

She wiped a bead of bodily fluid from her fair countenance.

"Taking the damn thing apart."

I surmised the day of reckoning for that old shed was at hand.

On the earth outside the shed, a pile of detritus was maturing as I watched. Plop! Another object flew out of the shed and contributed its body and soul to the pile. Dwelling on the assortment of metal, wood, plastic, and a few items of uncertain parentage constituting its architecture, I cast a bemused eye upon that growing pyramid.

Stuff. Years of stuff, once shiny new in some glittering emporium, now forlorn and unwanted.

"Here!" Pamela broke my reverie. "Take a look at this."

She handed me a cardboard box that had suffered the insult of whatever eats cardboard locked up in sheds. I peered within.

"It belonged to my grandmother," Pamela remarked before my eyes had a chance to focus.

Achieving, with some effort, due focus, that which "belonged to my grandmother"appeared to be a loose collection of gaily painted wood, some rusty chains, a tiny bird-like object, two ornate clock hands, and two rather heavy objects that appeared to be amateurish representations of pine cones. A few other items of mischievous character rattled around amidst the turmoil and chaos within the box. Counted among those were a few spiders. Greatly annoyed at the disturbance now rocking their world, they scurried off in a huff.

I wished them Godspeed. ("May God see that you prosper," from Middle English *spede*, third person singular present subjunctive of *speden*, "to prosper.")

"This seems to be a clock," observed I, "or at least at one time it was a clock."

"It is a cuckoo clock, and it belonged to my grandmother," she repeated for emphasis. She gave me a long look. As she is familiar with my peculiar background, her next utterance was not entirely unexpected. "Can you fix it?"

And so I found myself standing before a workbench in my garage, absorbing the disarming fact that I was in possession of an old, dismantled cuckoo clock. With trepidation, I inspected the collection of gears, pulleys, Bavarian rococo, and of course, one little itsy bitsy birdie. The prospect seemed melancholy.

Gathering my loins, I tenderly laid out what I had. Doing so brought me to consider the events leading up to this day. Back in the mists of time, someone had taken thought to contrive a clock that would announce the hour by a little bird poking out of a trapdoor whilst emitting earnest, if not stentorian, coos.

How such an unlikely act of artistic creation would ever have occurred to the mind of man or woman shall forever remain a mystery. Yet, the strangest ideas at times do bear fruit, as witnessed by Bosco, pole-dancing, religion, roulette wheels, the United States Supreme Court, French cuisine, Bella Abzug, and the mélange before me.

What to do?

Upon close inspection, I perceived two flutes, activated by bellows once linked ingeniously to the clockwork itself. Alas, the fabric of these bellows had long since succumbed to corrode-a-la-mode. The situation appeared grim.

Withholding judgment and invoking a spirit of experimental adventure, I activated the flutes by breathing through the holes once covered by the bellows. I was rewarded with a most satisfying pair of coos, at what seemed to my musical ear to be of appropriate timbre and at what I judged to be an interval of a robust subdominant fourth. "Coo," and then, "coo." They seemed like plaintive cries for rescue that stirred long-quiescent humanitarian emotions in my soul. Perhaps there is hope, thought I.

Turning to that infinite resource, the Internet, I was pleased to discover that cuckoo-clock repair is alive and well. I wouldn't have supposed that this arcana would justify an entire website dedicated to the preservation of old cuckoo clocks, but lo! There it was before me! It turns out that the number of distinct cuckoo clock entrails is manageably small, and replacement bellows for Pamela's grandmother's cuckoo clock were indeed available.

The clockwork movement itself, expressing a certain strength of character, is no delicate ladies' wristwatch. Yet, I feared the possibility that time and circumstance had inflicted internal insult. Exposed to the unforgiving elements as they had been, the entrails seemed constipated with entropic dirt glued to the gearing by spider industry.

The prospect of open-heart surgery filled me with dread. The back-plate seemed to be secured by four nuts and two tiny "C" rings. I could see the consequence of disassembly: a tabletop gaily festooned with festive gears happily rolling around in unfettered abandon. I would never get the damn thing back together.

Fortunately, such a frightful enterprise turned out to be not necessary. An overnight soaking in detergent, a strenuous hot-water rinsing, 10 minutes in a 200-degree oven, followed by judiciously placed drops of lubricating oil, and all seemed well. So far.

During my Internet research, I chanced upon a friendly sort of fellow who freely shared his expertise. In fact, he had produced a book on the care, feeding, and repair of cuckoo clocks. I developed a mental image of a white-haired *meister* somewhere in the Black Forest with rubber bands holding up his sleeves and wearing lederhosen, a green eyeshade, and half-moon glasses, while beaming grandfatherly smiles at neighborhood children. He would be inhabiting a cottage filled with cuckoo clocks and their parts. Through a window framed with ornate shutters and a tray of tulips, goats would be seen cavorting in a meadow.

An acquaintance who fancies himself a realist disagreed. He thought it more likely that I was communicating with an overseer in a cuckoo clock factory somewhere in Insanestan, whipping six-year-old children who worked fourteen hours a day assembling cuckoo clocks while surviving on a once-a-day bowl of thin lentil-gruel and a crust of dry bread. (The children, not the overseer.) This cannot be right. Miuccia Prada handbags? Yes. Nike athletic shoes? Yes. Cuckoo clocks? Surely no.

I am glad to say that, as I am writing this, Pamela's grandmother's cuckoo clock is sitting by my side, dutifully ticking away, and cooing the hour with enthusiasm.

I can report that the thorniest issue during reassembly was linking the clock movement to both coo flutes, to the rear gong, and to the bird itself. That bird linkage about drove me bats. I persevered because I understand that to achieve success when subduing any mechanical contrivance, it helps if you are smarter than it is. That happy state is not guaranteed, but in this case I managed it.

Finally, I must remark on the creative ingenuity exhibited by this device. All those wheels and gears and cams and linkages. All working synchronously, and cooing into the bargain.

A marvel indeed! I am impressed.

Crack

Amy E. Zajac

I sat tranquil on the bench since the time-out gave us a breather. The coach walked back from the pitcher's mound and the umpire yelled, "Batterup!" Tranquility lost, the shout was my cue to step in place as my team shouted, "Hit a homer, Amy, like last week. You can do it!"

Stepping up to home plate, I swung the bat, once with a miss and then a second time. *What could I have possibly been thinking, joining this team at 47? Softball at this age should be outlawed.*

"Strike two," the ump bellowed. I prayed to repeat last week's successful winning home run, which kept us in the finals.

That moment was still vivid in my mind's eye. Heart pounding I blew past first, rounded second and then dived head first with my arms reaching for third base. The dirt so dry and powdery, its granules buried me up to my shoulders as I came to a stop in a dust cloud. I nursed both black and blue arms with ice and bandages all week, but I was safe. Then I endured the dozens of comments at the office, "Wow Amy, I didn't know you played softball." "Tough weekend, Amy, what does the other guy look like!"

The pitcher wound up and fired.

Keep focused...I can't disappoint all these wonderful people, my church team, who helped me so much this year. *Oh great, sweat is in my eyes.* I raised my hand for a time-out; I needed to mop my forehead.

Stepping back into place, the steady ball streamed by me in a flash. "Ball one," the umpire yelled.

Oh man, I can't believe I missed that one; just not paying attention yet, but at least it was off to the side.

My team and the crowd watched in silence.

Come on; play like you did when you were 10 years old. Remember the feeling and the applause when the opposing teams watched the balls flying over their heads as your homers disappeared over the back fence.

"Ball two," he yelled again.

Oh, no…what's happening. I'm lost in my 47-ness.

I tighten my grip and focus.

The windup.

The pitch.

Here it comes. Watch… watch…

Not yet.

One more second.

CRACK!

The crowd was on its feet!

The Haven

Philip R. Pryde

(For the 50th reunion of the Amherst College class of '59.)

Once upon a midnight dreary, while I pondered, weak and
    weary,
Over pints of grog and boring homework chore,
While I nodded, nearly napping, suddenly there came a tapping,
As of someone gently rapping, rapping at my Frat room door.
"Tis some piteous Frosh," I muttered, "tapping at my chamber
    door,
          Only this and nothing more."
Presently the knock grew stronger, hesitating then no longer,
"Sir,"said I, "or madam, truly your forgiveness I implore;
But the fact is I was napping, and so gently you came rapping.
And so faintly you came tapping, tapping at my Frat room door,
That I scarce was sure I heard you." Here I opened wide the
    door—
          The Dean's stern glare clean through me tore.
"Son," said he, "you're in grave danger, one to which I am no
    stranger,
For beer and long procrastination, means you'll study here no
    more.

You were not reading, nor just snoozing; obviously, you were
boozing,

And I can tell you, you're in danger, danger you'll be shown the
door.

A homeless bum without a friend, a long forgotten flop of yore;
And you'll study here at Amherst — Nevermore!"

Pale was I with limbs all shaking, drinks to sober up now taking,

Swearing on my Letter I'd be better than before.

Turning pen and ink to essay, readying my brain for test day,

Once again a model student, student virtues all restored,

Able now to graduate, yes, Amherst sheepskin now in store —
One could ask for nothing more.

Then came the years in quick profusion; time seems just a cruel
illusion,

As we await what fickle fate might have for each of us in store.

And while we sought career admirement, some spoilsport soon
said, "Retirement!"

Ponder now life's paid toil ending! Yet, our type-A genes implore

How still to serve our friends and nation, thrilling new worlds to
explore —
Do what we choose, the rest ignore!

Then one day, too soon to mention, a purple letter grabs
attention:
Saying, yes, we graduated — *fifty* years before!

Setting aside our disbelief (but still we breathe — that's a relief!),

Our traveling gear we now make ready, ready for the trip once
> more
To our Haven, on the hill, that overlooks the Valley floor —
> Friends and memories to restore.
With joy, the grad now contemplates tall tales to thrill his old
> classmates,
> > Thinking, drinking, tinkering, as before.
By plane and train we soon arrive — at Amherst, still robust, alive,
Inspiring yet new generations, and therein making us still more
Enriched by *our* collective efforts, proud of what we've striven
> for.
> > Here's to coming back in fifty more!
> > Cheers!

The Woods

Alan Converse

They beckoned from outside my window. I peeked out at them before I went to sleep. We planned to hunt in them in the morning. A hunter's dream, the fall woods, flecked with colors of red, yellow, and orange, awaited us. Squirrels, rabbits, and maybe even deer might fall to our arrows. We planned to meet at dawn and creep into the trees, like Indians.

Now they seemed dark, cold, and foreboding. The sunlit warmth of the day gone, shadows moved in the bushes as moonlight created bizarre shapes. Dangers existed in those woods; unspecified fears whispered beware, as if the light breeze itself were speaking. What predators stalked the tangle of undergrowth? I pictured wolves lying in wait for us when we pushed off into the underbrush. It would be a steep climb at first, the brambles and musty wet leaves slowing our progress.

We expected to climb right through the thickest part of the woods, avoiding the path and sneaking up on the game unseen. We would move slowly, placing our feet with care so as not to break a twig or make a sound that might expose us. If we moved this way, we knew surprise would be on our side, and we would hear the wolves before they could attack us, leaving no way for them to drag us out of the jumbled thicket.

The threat lurked in that first clearing, where the game gathered. The wolves assembled nearby, waiting to attack us. *No, I told myself, no wolves existed in the woods*, but as I peered at the darkness from my bedroom window, I wasn't so sure.

Next morning and Johnny Kuhn stood at the door. Kuhnnie shivered outside, pale and scared. We looked at the woods. We left our homemade bows and arrows on the porch and scrambled inside to eat Mom's pancakes.

Single Father's Day

Gary Winters

Seven years old, my daughter, Tanis, went from a maternal to a paternal lifestyle, just like that.

I dressed her in jeans and T-shirts, the prevailing Berkeley dress code. She had all the street names memorized in a week. She climbed trees, walked to school holding her Yamaha guitar by the neck, and played songs for her girlfriends during recess. After school they'd descend like a band of marauding midgets on the coffeehouse I frequented, so they could swipe powdered chocolate off the steamed-milk foam on my cappuccino with their grubby little fingers.

But she couldn't bring herself to call me Daddy without giving a little grunt to let me know it was an effort. One day she forgot to grunt first. She immediately realized what she'd done — called me Daddy without grunting first — so she grunted after she said Daddy. She looked out of the corner of her eye to see if I'd noticed. I didn't worry about it. Her best friend, Heather, the feisty daughter of a doctor, always called me "Dadso."

One of the strongest emotions I ever had was when I took a good look at my daughter and got the feeling — not a thought, a tangible feeling, something that had its own existence inside me —

that there was no question I would give my life in a nanosecond to protect her from harm.

My daughter stayed with me for two years. When I knew she was all right I placed her with her maternal grandparents. She was their first grandchild, sort of like their fifth child. They had raised four girls and her grandmother could teach her things I didn't have a clue about. A grand piano and a fireplace adorned her spacious bedroom, with a redwood deck that looked out over Carmel Valley in central California. I arranged for her to share in the inheritance of the estate equally with the other daughters. That was a crucial break in our relationship. I knew that.

How could my daughter not blame me for the way things turned out. In her seven-year-old mind she must have wondered what things would be like if I hadn't divorced her mother.

Who knows what she thought. Tanis did all right, ending up with a graduate degree in telecommunications from the University of Southern California. I congratulated her, then said, "I didn't know they had a degree in telephone."

John and the
Great Virginia Ham Swindle

Dave Feldman

At that time, the early 1950s, the going rate for hiring reporters off the street was $50 a week.

We got John Riddick for $40, because he had no experience. And he was hungry.

John had a brilliant mind. He was close to getting his PhD in New York, but gave it up to wander out West. Among many things, John was a wanderer. Also a ladies' man, a confirmed bachelor, and the sponsor of what we at the *Tucson Daily Citizen* called the Great Annual Virginia Ham Swindle.

It wasn't really a swindle. It was just the way John could get back to his roots in Virginia each summer, by Greyhound bus. It worked this way: John would ask each of us in the newsroom if we wanted a real, smoked ham. Straight from Virginia, and at a good price, paid in advance. I think it may have been $15.

We all chipped in, which provided John with the round-trip bus fare, enough money for the hams, and a little profit. So a swindle it wasn't—we just liked calling it that.

John would ride the Greyhound to Virginia—a trip that would have obliterated the rest of us—spend time with the mother he adored, then return to Tucson with the 20 or so hams.

Most of the hams were in the baggage compartment, but he kept one or two inside the bus—I don't know why—and their odor, or fragrance, as the case may be, must have engulfed the passengers all the way from Virginia to Arizona.

John was so passionate about the hams as he delivered them that we had to be profuse in our thanks. Actually, they were tasty.

John was passionate about many things. The future of journalism, for one. He and I would talk for hours about writing. "It's going to get more personal," he would say. "This stuff of impersonal reporting will change. It has to. We're turning off the damned readers." (Poor John. He must be spinning wildly in his final resting place at the state of newspapers today.)

John Riddick was also passionate about the ladies. He had an advantage, being exceedingly handsome. Looked like a young James Mason, if you can remember the movies back in the early 1950s. And John wasn't shy about quietly hitting on some of the reporters' wives, when their husbands were not around.

When John came aboard, I was the junior member of a three-man sports department, so I took him under my wing so he could be the junior member. He didn't know diddly about sports writing, or newspapers, but he learned quickly. In fact, he graduated from the sports department (known as the Toy Store or the Playpen) before I did.

On the news side, John continued to develop as a writer. He won a couple of prizes in the state press club contests. Then I left sports and was learning to be a reporter, too, so we had a lot of talks.

When I became the assistant city editor, going over most of the reporters' copy, I had another chance to work with John.

With that inquisitive mind, he was an excellent interviewer. But writing didn't come easy. I can still see him pacing up and down in the newsroom, brushing back his hair with one hand while trying to think of a lead for his story.

"John," I said once, "I like the way you covered that congressman's speech. But you cannot, really cannot, write an entire story in direct quotes. That's 18 paragraphs in direct quotes, and nothing else. The readers want some background." He marched back to his typewriter and repaired the story.

John had a steady girlfriend, Mary Anne, a bright and attractive young woman. He once said, in an offhand sort of way, that they would make love all night, then argue all the next day about who was the better lover. Mary Anne, after waiting and waiting for him to propose, finally gave up, realizing that he would never marry. He never did. Some of the reporters' wives tried to analyze that, the consensus being that he was still too attached to his mother.

The phrase Southern gentleman comes to mind. John was ever polite. "It's a damned shame the kids of today don't have to say 'Sir' or 'Ma'am' or 'Thank you,' " he told me. "You're not going to be talking back to people when you call them 'Sir.' "

He visited our house often. Once, my wife and I played our favorite record, songs by Tom Lehrer, for John. He howled aloud at the satire, most of it wise. Lehrer poked fun at the Old West, at bullfights, at masochism, and at many cultural icons. "The Vatican Rag" was one of our favorites.

But then the parody about the South came on: "I Wanna Go Back to Dixie." It was bad enough when Lehrer sang about "whuppin' slaves and sellin' cotton." But that was followed by: "I wanna talk with Southern gentlemen, and put that white sheet on again. I ain't seen one good lynchin' in years."

John's earlier guffaws turned to stone-dead silence.

It was a mistake, on our part. John was a true Southern gentleman. And one who would abhor lynchings.

When the Vietnam War came along, John was adamant about covering it firsthand. He pleaded with the newspaper to send him as a correspondent. The paper said no. So John went anyway, and arrived there just in time for the Tet Offensive by the Communist troops. We did pay him for his dispatches.

After the war, John returned to Tucson and worked as a freelancer, learning to write longer pieces for magazines. But Vietnam had been a treacherous place. He had picked up a serious bug and spent months in the hospital, then passed away.

It was no way for a Southern gentleman to leave us.

Men and Balls

Diana Avery Amsden

What is it with men and balls?

Little girls play jacks. Some women play ball games, but not in the numbers or with the enthusiasm men do.

Men like balls, from marbles to giant beach balls.

They like to bounce them, chase them, dodge them, dribble them, juggle them, kick them, shoot them, drive them under hoops and through wickets, knock them into pockets, putt them into holes, roll them toward pins, run with them, throw them through baskets, and catch and toss them with cestas.

Above all, they like to *hit* balls. They hit them across nets, hit them with bats, clubs, cues, mallets, paddles, rackets, sticks, fists, hips, palms, rumps, and even heads.

No other primate exhibits comparable behavior. The Khoisan of South Africa, probably the least-changed descendants of the earliest humans, use wild melons for balls. The longest isolated human group, the Australian aborigines, had balls, as did ancient Egypt, China, and pre-Columbian Mexico.

For fascination with balls to be encoded in male genes, it must have conferred a survival or mating advantage. What did our male ancestors roll or toss or bat? Skulls?

I may never understand what it is with men and balls.

The only balls I like are held in elegant ballrooms, where my beautiful ball gown swirls as I waltz.

Leaving Solitude

Bob Doublebower

Jerry drove like a bat outta hell. He drove like that without provocation …just because. He drove like a bat outta hell, that is, until he reached the Interstate. He could see it crawl at its best 10-to-20 on through the low hills to the north and no doubt over at least one ridgeline past them, if history was any guide.

"Goddamn Friday traffic." Jerry cursed the 'get-out-of-towners' for their ill-timed use of the highway, even though, of course, he was one.

His refuge lay beyond that far ridgeline. This goddamn traffic ("…goddamn get-out-of-towners..") stood as a barrier to getting there, but was, all in all, a small price to pay for the weekend away. He'd worked all week. He deserved it. His family, oh crap, would be up on Saturday, noonish, but tonight he had the run of the place. You know, get things running. Make it nice for when they get there.

"Goddamn traffic !" This time the imprecation must have worked, because on the first upgrade past the low hills, things thinned out. He made it to the turnoff a scant two hours later.

It wasn't like the place lay forlorn. They got up at least every other week, with the full two-day agenda of cookouts, kids splashing and screaming and the never-ending list of little fix-it items. Jerry had his reasons for getting here early. Ahh, the Friday night solitude.

He'd swear it's what kept his brain unscrambled, kept it able to focus. Some go in for loud — loud casinos, loud bars with loud music — as their way to keep the cargo netting tight, brainwise. That's a sea where treading water is easy, at least for a while. So go in for intrigue — affairs, vendettas, and such. You must stay focused to play that game, or else. But none of these for Jerry. He liked solitude.

He literally burst through the back screen door and out onto the deck. He slowly turned with his arms outstretched…well, no, not really, but it looked for all the world as though he wanted to.

Their lot was narrow, by lake standards, but so was the house. Jerry took the side path out to the street on the north side, chosen over the one just like it on the south side, only because the chair cushion bin was there. First things first.

Jerry settled in. It was about nine, and a smattering of crickets were out. Darkness had crept in, revealing stars and not much of a moon. Wind so light only the most fainthearted of leaves knew it.

And so he sat and gazed at the sky for a while in all its pinpoint mystery, then at the house's back wall with its dull-lit window squares, then at the roofline against the trees, so omnipresent it seemed odd for a house to be here. He gazed at the corner of the deck where it opened onto the side path. Whatever faint light bathed the deck soon evaporated into pitch black as the path led streetward. The wind hadn't picked up, so the faint brush and twig sounds he heard he wrote off to critters. The lake shore had no shortage of them, and their noises always spooked him a little. In the darkness of the path, it surprised him to still see some distinct leaves — mid-sized and oval and green.

These must have been among the stouter ones because, when a zephyr rolled through, the pair didn't move. No, wait, there were four of them, he could see. What plant was that? He tried to recall all the bushes down that side. The leaves stayed stock still. He hadn't noticed them on his earlier trip to and from the cushion bin.

Jerry got up, went into the kitchen, and came back with two fingers of scotch in a grubby water glass. The leaves were still there — still oval and still green against the darkness — except the two that had appeared lower to the ground and nearer the house had switched sides with the higher, outer pair. That jump-started a small trickle of anxiety that Jerry found hard to explain. He sipped his scotch and stayed very still. Another breeze came in off the lake and still the leaves remained unmoved.

Then, as he sat and stared, one leaf of the upper pair moved toward, then disappeared behind, the other. In about four heartbeats, the other pair did the same, only opposite. Without trying, Jerry's left hand set up a ripple on the surface of the drink it held. He sank a little lower in his chair. Leaves, of course, but such a lively green in that lightless way.

It was about then he noticed the new silence. Whatever small animals he'd thought he'd heard earlier were now long gone. Even the oval, green leaves, when they turned back to their original position facing Jerry, did so without so much as a rustle.

Jerry sat there slowly losing his certainty of things. To make matters worse, the leaves that once slid one behind the other and back, did so again and again, only at irregular intervals and varying speeds in the dead-calm air.

When he had first seen them earlier, he had the notion to go over and swat them down, take a clipper to them. Those leaves didn't belong there. But now he felt a reluctance born of prudence. Way down deep inside, he welcomed it. Prudence and fear. He drained the last of his glass.

Jerry wondered if, over the years, he'd ever been watched, and what that must feel like. The thought immobilized him.

The leaves' queer movements went on for the better part of an hour, though their frequency fell off markedly in the last half. Jerry's glass had long since slipped from his fingers and smashed on the deck's hard surface. Scotch was, truly, the last thing on his mind.

Then the leaves rotated in something that looked like the opposite direction, and were seen no more. The foliage rustled.

Jerry sat there on the deck 'til well past three in the morning. It takes time to rethink your love of solitude.

One Flower Gone

Joseph Bonpensiero

Time has flown leaving so few memories of you,
    Samantha my flower, thoughts of you keep me blue.
Time rushed by; decades withered me at last,
    but my mind, ever sharp, will not forget the past.

English Stout and sweet tart to celebrate your birth
    we savored the thought—happy hearts—silly mirth.
For nine months, we sang, laughing out loud
    A new babe is coming, from God in the clouds.

The bassinet so bright, your mother so happy,
    excited at last to make me a pappy.
Dear infant, sweet baby, how pretty in pink,
    your room is ready, new clothes, toys and sink.

Things here are joyful, they're light and so gay,
    soon, maybe tomorrow will be your birthday.
Dear sweetness, little child, oh love of my life,
    how could we know then a future with strife?

A car from the village going oh, much too fast,
    a swerve, an impact—all destroyed—too good to last.
The doctor in blue gown, passed you to me
    all swaddled in blankets, I could not help see.

The black of your hair and your pug little nose,
    tender sweet lips and luscious pink toes.
Oh, such a beauty but I'm never to see,
    my sweet daughter, this child, growing up with me.

Tiny white casket, she so alone and so cold,
    this babe and I—my child—with no God to scold.
Misty the morn, dew blankets English yew and fir,
    no birds today singing, just me alone here with her.

No peace, no, not ever, she laid to rest there,
    a plot in damp ground—Woodbridge Town Square.
A wife and a daughter, a family no more
    Only sorrowful memories—does this even the score?

Bitter gifts that you gave, oh god—and for naught,
    You left me alone, heartbroken, distraught.
Who gathered this Flower, I cry to the sky.
    Deity above—silent, there was no reply.

Once Mine

Margaret Coughlin

Marian Madison parked in front of 2436 Whipple Street. Memories of eighteen years in her Indiana home combined with a few tears so, before leaving her car, she wiped her eyes with a tissue.

In the chilly March air, the petite twenty-six year-old brunette fastened her down jacket as she stood on the sidewalk. The sales agent hadn't arrived, so Marian checked her phone for messages, then gazed at the houses to the left and right. *I'd forgotten,* she mused, *that they're all so similar.*

The winds had increased, forcing dark clouds to mass overhead. No longer reveling in the winter morning sun, the house looked like what it truly was: an old, one-story, dull, red-brick bungalow, with patches of gray trim on the bay-windowed front. A few fliers skittered on the three concrete steps leading to the front porch.

An older woman, elegantly dressed in a brown, tailored pantsuit, approached, breaking into her thoughts.

"Sorry to be late, Ms. Madison. There aren't many parking spaces here." Holding out her hand, Katherine Barnes said, "So this is your family home."

"Yes. My father moved us here when I was about two. When

mother passed, five years ago, Dad moved to Florida." Marian glanced up at the house. *I felt lonely. Even though we talked often.*

She looked back to Ms. Barnes. "He rented the house for income. But he died recently."

"I'm sorry. Do you have any other family?"

"Yes." Marian paused. "I have a half-brother, eight years older. My mother's son, John, from her first marriage, but, unfortunately, we've lost touch." She eyed the dreary yard, thinking, *While I was growing up, Johnny was so much fun. I missed him after he left.*

They stepped onto the porch.

"I haven't been inside for a while," Marian said, producing a key from a ring. The two pushed open the heavy, scarred door to enter into the living room.

And Marian's past.

The clouds created an interior dark enough for Marian to switch on the overhead light.

"I can see this is a typical twenties style," Ms. Barnes said. "The fireplace with shelves on either side and small windows above. And the dining room through that arch."

Marian didn't heed the agent's quiet comments. She heard, instead, her unhappy, non-musical hours of practicing on the piano, that used to be in the corner near the archway. *And those fireplace shelves look lonesome,* she reflected. *Mom had filled them with books because she loved to read.*

In the dining-room, Marian remembered, *All those nights when Johnny and I couldn't have dessert because we still had vegetables on our plates!*

Marian strove to bury her emotions as she continued the tour. "The kitchen leads to the back porch. Dad turned this porch into another room."

"I see," Ms. Barnes said. "Now, let's return to the kitchen."

The women walked around. "This is a pleasant room, Marian. But much of it is dated. The cabinets, the sink area. Perhaps a bit of modernizing...."

The rest of the walk-through resonated with further repair ideas from Ms. Barnes, who was unaware that, in the smallest bedroom, Marian was distracted through recalling her youth.

Those walls had eavesdropped on her joyful times, and the worst, many shared with Patty Nelson, her best school friend.

Ms. Barnes completed her assessment of the older-model house, then offered another suggestion.

"Our office can connect you with a remodeler, Ms. Madison. He's experienced and will understand what you'll need."

Marian said, "That's fine." She removed a key from the ring. "Here's a spare key for you."

At the front door, the agent gave her the contractor's card. She promised to check back within a few days.

Before closing the door, Marian turned to view, once more, the empty rooms. *I know I want to sell it, but it's like selling my memories.* After a few moments, she sighed deeply. *Well, it'll be difficult, but I'll try to move on.*

Then Marian locked up her house and drove along the block, carefully surveying the other buildings. *I can see at least two houses are renovated. There is, indeed, gentrification going on.*

During the following week, Marian thought seriously about the problem. She understood that with repairs the house would garner better offers. But the costs might hurt her financially, and she didn't like loans. Finally, she made a decision.

She e-mailed Ms. Barnes to have that contractor examine the property and furnish bids that would reflect modest renovations. And, most importantly, their prices. Then, she would weigh all the aspects of his plans. Marian included her available dates for the consultation.

*

On the last Saturday morning in March, Marian returned to her family home. Entering the living room, she saw a broad-shouldered man rise from one of a pair of folding chairs. His shaggy brown hair made her think, *He's young. How could he be so experienced?*

"Jack Donaldson, Ms. Madison," he said. "Please sit."

She noted his rolling briefcase and friendly smile. Their initial conversation went well, although his eyeglasses occasionally slipping down his nose amused her. Picking up a clipboard with attached sheets, he said he would explain his designs as they explored each room. "Let's start with this one, the living room. And the fireplace wall."

Marian noticed his surreptitiously watching her, not the walls under discussion.

"You know that any results of this will probably---"

Marian interrupted. "How long have you been a contractor here, Mr. Donaldson?"

Jack stopped speaking, then said, "About four years here, Mar-. Uh-Ms. Madison. Before that, I worked for ten years in Evansville."

Marian studied Jack. *Something about him….*

Jack smiled at her. "I enjoyed thinking up ideas for your house. I was raised in one like it. I know about its potential changes. Have you been living here?"

Marian explained how she moved away after college and her father began renting the house. "Dad took care of the tenants. I only helped with the financial end of things and at tax time."

After listening to Jack's plans for the living room and kitchen, Marian said, "Could we stop right here? My head is spinning from all these changes."

"Sure. But can we go into the enclosed porch before leaving?"

Marian said, "What do you have in mind, Mr. Donaldson? It's just a big room we used a lot."

She watched Jack move thoughtfully around the room. He rubbed certain window frames, smiled, and patted the door. More smiles.

"What are you doing, Mr. Donaldson?"

He turned, pushed up his glasses again, and faced her. "I guess you were too young to remember how your dad and I worked together on this room."

Marian stopped. "Johnny?"

She stared at him, then said, "Oh, my goodness."

She moved closer. "Oh, that's why I thought I knew you. You always had trouble with glasses."

Jack smiled and put out his hand. "It's been a long time, Marian." She took his hand and he tenderly guided her back to the living room.

As they sat, Marian said, "You ran away. And never told me you were leaving." She slapped his hand. "Or said goodbye. That was mean, Johnny!"

"I know, Marian. You were only a child while Dad spent so much time educating me about carpentry. And then, after high school, I felt I had to leave home." He leaned toward her. "I realize this is a lot for you to handle. But I'd like to be friends once more."

He spoke quietly. "Would you like a cup of coffee at the Koffee Kup? It'll help me attempt to explain."

Marian agreed.

When they arrived, Jack led Marian to a booth and returned a few minutes later with two lattes.

Marian said, "You left home, Johnny. I never saw you again!" She tried to lift the cup. "It's almost more than I can take in."

Her hands trembled so, Jack reached over to fold his hands around Marian's, his eyes soft with care. "You know, earlier I almost called you Marian. Didn't you wonder at that?"

"No, I guess I was so overwhelmed talking about the remodeling, and feeling sad at the same time. I kept wondering if I knew you. Your glasses reminded me of someone. But I couldn't think who."

My funny, delightful Johnny. Here, she thought. *No, he's Jack now.*

"Your name is Donaldson now?" She asked.

"I'm using my own father's name. Why did I leave? Mother kept insisting that I go to college. I couldn't stand it anymore. All I wanted to be was a carpenter like your dad."

When she started to cry, Jack stood. "Come here, Marian." He pulled her up and wrapped his arms around her. They hugged, oblivious to everyone.

She sniffled, used a paper napkin to wipe her face, then, laughed, too.

"Oh, Johnny. You're back!"

The Gambler

Carolyn Jaynes

From *Sprinkles from Heaven*

I met a gambler with a losing hand
Who clung to me like a dying man
He played upon my true compassion
I took him in (in sympathetic fashion)

He lost all the money he had for our rent
Then made up stories on how it was spent
He lied every time he moved his lips
Denying the slots at his fingertips

I crave escape from this survival rut
I tiptoe on egg shells, knots in my gut
How could I be so naïve not to see
All this time he was deceiving me

All his bets he thought were a shoe-in
'Til I asked him to leave to avoid complete ruin
The Casino strategy: *Treat him like a Star*
How regal are you when you sleep in your car?

Gamblers Anonymous, we went to a meeting
They welcomed us with a warm greeting
I talked about this man I love very much
Who's in so much pain and out of touch

Now all I can do is stay busy and wait
He'll either quit gambling or we'll separate
Is he going to stop now, placing his bets
Or leave me alone to pay all our debts?

I know he's feeling incredible shame
He hides out, avoids it, and shifts all the blame
Penniless, broken, all he owns is his name
What now is rock bottom, was once just a *game*.

Mama's Addiction ... and Mine

Marcia Buompensiero

Five is early for addiction. Everyone knows that. Experts say that psychological dependence is what spawns craving beyond all reason. That's how it was for me. Coffee, not simply its fragrance and substance, but the ritual of drinking it, became mine.

But, before coffee, there was the beginning.

Mother and Father were out of the picture — another story for another time. I lived with my grandmother. She worked, so childcare was required. I bounced from one babysitter to another. None were satisfactory, not for grandmother or me. Without playmates, I retreated to picture books and the friendship of imaginary friends. We conversed regularly and at odd hours, day and night — these playmates of my creation. This worried grandmother.

Life with a grandparent is like missing a link to the last generation — a time-warp chromosome deleted from your DNA. Grandmother didn't traffic with psychologists. The pesky social trends in child-rearing psychology, the permissive nurturing of developing psyches — all pretty much ignored. She believed that children should follow rules. That simple paradigm made sense if you lived through a global Depression and two world wars. Luckily, after several sitter mismatches, divine intervention led grandmother to the perfect daytime keeper for her precocious grandchild. Her name was Mrs. Maestro. Thus, I was entrusted to a sixty-five-year old Sicilian grandmother. Within minutes of our introduction, she had me calling her "Mama."

Perched on a canyon rim in Mission Hills, the Maestro home became my enchanted playground. Below it, wild grasses and eucalyptus rimmed a pen where goats were kept. The Maestros borrowed a neighbor's dirt plot, where fallow ground was transformed into a garden paradise. Green leafy greens teepee towers grew heavy with long fingered pole beans. Tomato bushes glowed with plump red fruit as big as Christmas ornaments. Parsley, basil, rosemary, and thyme perfumed the air.

Under Mama's Sicilian touch, everything flourished. Her kitchen bustled with gastronomic delights — enough to fill volumes of cookbooks.

"Everything homemade!" was her mantra, and she taught me what she knew. Crusty artisan bread was baked in a clay-and-brick oven in her patio. Chickens were raised. Goats bred. And, like everything that flourished in her garden, she raised me.

Mornings, I gathered eggs, naming each hen for an imaginary friend. I soon learned that talking to chickens rather than to invisible pals is less worrisome to adults. I milked Bella the goat and strained her frothy gift through layers of cheesecloth. A warm glass of Bella's milky broth with a hunk of crusty bread drizzled in olive oil — gastro-ecstasy.

But it was not the food, nor the mini-farm, that hooked me. It began innocently enough. A fragrance, a taste — a connection to some deep craving that became an obsession.

It began at seven-fifteen sharp every morning when grandmother dropped me off at the Maestro home. "Papa" Maestro, a gardener at the Hotel del Coronado, had cranked up his old Chevy and rumbled off to work before dawn. He'd return just before grandmother picked me up after her workday. Thus, alone with Mama, my day began.

Hoisting my overall cuffs above my high-top Buster Browns to avoid tripping, I climbed the twenty-five steps to their Craftsman bungalow and slipped in through the unlocked back door. No one locked doors in those days; trust was unwritten and understood.

Mama, still asleep, left the coffee-making to me. Coffee basic was an aluminum pot from Hammond's Five and Dime. That was it. I'd dump the used grounds from the last pot of coffee into a container. Later, they would be sprinkled under the hydrangeas in the garden to keep the soil acidic and the blossoms an electric shade of violet. Next, the perforated sieve basket and lid were rinsed under cold water. Soap was never used — ever! After filling the pot with water to the top indentation — 3 — for the number of cups, five heaping tablespoons of coffee were added to the basket. The lid, with its hollow glass knob, was fitted into place and the pot was set to boil over the gas burner. I watched as water percolated up into the tiny glass bubble. When it turned a rich, dark brown, it was done. The grounds were allowed to settle before pouring.

The black lacquered tray held two china cups with matching saucers. Hand-painted purple flowers trimmed in gold made them special. Sugar and creamer bowls and two demitasse spoons were added. Fragrant hazelnut biscotti were placed on a matching dessert plate. (Mama said that for the heart to be sweet, the day must begin with biscotti.)

Next, steaming coffee was poured and the tray and I headed down the hallway to Mama's bedroom. Placing it on her nightstand, I would touch her lightly. She pretended to be asleep, but I suspect that she listened to every movement I made, ticking off steps to ensure they were followed — to the letter.

Then, down on my knees and onto my stomach. Scooting under the bed, I'd retrieve the bottle of anisette — a potent licorice-flavored liqueur used in Sicilian cookie making. I measured one full bottle-cap into Mama's coffee and half of that into mine. Two spoonfuls of sugar in each cup and enough rich cream to turn the brew pale khaki.

"*Buon giorno!*" Mama would say, sitting up, arranging her satin bedjacket and reclining against the pillows.

"*Bwan-jor-no,*" I would reply, carefully mimicking her accent to get it right.

Thus, our day began.

As the fragrance of anisette-infused coffee curled around me, so did Mama's stories about growing up in turn-of-the-century Sicily. Like Scheherazade's tales of *One Thousand and One Nights*, Mama's were exotic with intrigue and wild with romance. Vignettes told from the villager's perspective — simple, yet poignant, to anchor reality. This is one such story. My favorite.

"In Sicily," she said, between sips of coffee and a bite of biscotti, "no marriage unless your papa and mama approve."

"What if they don't?" I said, savoring my brew.

"Then, you plan," she said and winked. "When a suitor asked for my hand, Papa said, 'No!'"

Another bite of biscotti followed by a question, "What did you do, Mama?"

"Me? Nothing. What could I do? I was fourteen. But, in my town, there is a custom. If the girl is kidnapped by a suitor, they must marry."

"Kidnapped!" This word I knew from a picture book. Visions of frightened children flung into the midst of scruffy villains flashed before me. I sat up straight. Fear picked at my nerves.

"One day," Mama continued, "my sister Anna and I were walking back home from baking bread in the village ovens. As we passed by the seawall, a bandit jumped out from behind a bush. He grabbed the loaves I carried and gave them to Anna — all but one. Then, he told her to run home. He lifted me up onto the back of his donkey and off we went — into the mountains."

"Did you fight him?" I brandished my little clenched fists.

"*Cara mia!*" she laughed. "No worry. The bandit was — *Papa!*

"Ooooh," I said, nodding. Instant relief and a big smile.

"When he brought me home the next day, he told my papa we must marry."

The dilemma now tied up neatly, my imagination was free to run ahead, painting the landscape in the joyous colors of a big celebration. Since I had no concept of a poor Sicilian village wedding, naturally, in storybook style I saw a great hall awash in golden candlelight, a huge feast laid out, and ladies in satin and lace laughing and dancing with dashing princes.

I pointed to Mama and Papa's wedding photograph in the bubble-glass frame, he so regal — a prince; she, demure, beautiful. "And you wore that lacy dress?"

"*Si, si,*" she said. "It was my mama's gown." She closed her eyes, the better to remember, I think. "We had a big *festa* with a roasted goat. There was wine. Music. Dancing."

I had trouble envisioning a goat roasting on a spit in the middle of my grand hall but I improvised. Then, it occurred to me that Mama was leaving out an important part of the story.

"Mama," I asked, "what happened in the mountains?"

She was quiet. I was sure she was trying to remember, since it was so very long ago. Then, she smiled.

"He made me coffee," she said and winked, "with anisette."

*

Coffee with Mama Maestro defined life's magic. It gave light and life to worlds and ideas. It spoke of old-fashioned grit. About squeezing the sweet from the sour when life tossed you lemons. About intertwined destinies. It touched a neglected child with a lonely woman's love. Mama Maestro is gone. But coffee remains. It was the elixir of seduction for Mama and me. It unfurled my imagination. It caressed my heart.

It does. Still.

Eric

Lawrence Carleton

"I've moved out, Eric," she said. He didn't see her until she spoke. The place was dark, crowded and noisy. The band was playing something he didn't recognize. The overhead TVs had a hockey game on: Red Wings against Ducks.

She didn't look up. Head down in front of him, she shook her long, dark ponytail and continued. "You have no ambition. You need to make an effort to make something of yourself, and I have to do the same for me. The sex was beyond fantasy, I give you that; but there has to be more to a relationship. Here is your key." She leaned against him as she fished out the key, and when he didn't move, felt along his jeans and pushed it into his left pocket. She started to look up. He got the slightest flash of almond eyes before she thought better of it and stared down again.

"If I kiss you good-bye we'll end up doing it right here on the floor. I'll just go. This is farewell." She pushed against his chest with her long, slender fingers as she turned away from him. He watched her perfect butt sway into the crowd and disappear, then followed her ponytail to the exit. He saw her face in profile after she turned to the right, not looking back, and disappeared at the end of the window.

He wanted to follow her out into the night. He wanted to

catch up to her under a light post, and hold her to him with everything he had. He wanted to look deeply into those bright eyes and tell her, "I'll change: change for you, change for us." He wanted to take her home and promise her everything with every ounce of honesty he could call up as he explored every part of her slim, athletic body, and see those bright eyes look into his with trust and acceptance.

The band started another tune. The Red Wings scored.

Someone thumped his arm, then apologized. "Sorry, Dude. You look exactly like someone I know."

"No problem," he replied without turning toward him. "I get that a lot." He just stood there, retracing in his mind her path through the crowd, out the door, and into the night. He was not Eric, and he didn't know her name.

*

Poor guy, I thought. He has no idea what hit him. Of course Claire saw me, I was standing right there. This was her way of telling me off without actually confronting me, never mind the collateral damage. I guess I should buy the man a beer. At least get my key back.

The Stained Glass Woman

Diana Avery Amsden

1. TWINS

"A lie that is half-truth is the darkest of all lies."

(Alfred, Lord Tennyson)

Genevieve Yoder Esmand lay exhausted on the delivery room table in the Vorbeck Maternity Hospital in suburban Los Angeles. The doctor and nurse laid two newborn infants, bathed and warmly swaddled, beside their mother. The doctor looked down at his patient with the awestruck expression that had illuminated his face at her first appointment. At Genevieve's second, the nurse had whispered to her, "Doc and I think your face is the most angelic we've ever seen."

Genevieve had practiced in front of her dressing-table mirror the beatific smile she had seen a few months earlier on her sister Louise's face after giving birth. Genevieve looked up at her doctor with the smile of a tired angel who needs rest.

The doctor beamed down on her. "When two babies must share quarters Mother Nature intended for only one, one twin can get shortchanged. I'm happy to say your babies are perfectly healthy and weigh the same down to the half ounce."

She glowed up at him, gratified to see that he looked

enchanted all over again.

"Why isn't your husband here?"

"Fred's out of town on a job." The Great Depression was in its fifth year.

"At a time like this?"

"We need the money."

When Genevieve was finally alone in her own room, the seraphic smile vanished. Remembering her secret marriage and brief honeymoon, she smirked at the contrast with her parents' traditional Amish celibate honeymoon, based on the apocryphal *Book of Tobit.*

Fred had insisted she get a diaphragm. She did, but she didn't use it. She wanted to get pregnant immediately so that when Fred Esmand's wealthy family found out about the marriage, they couldn't easily annul it. *It's easier to get forgiveness than permission.*

After the doctor told Genevieve she carried twins, she had thought, *Oh, for Sam Hill! I need only one brat to keep Fred from divorcing me. I won't raise two!*

She had gone home and told Fred, "The doctor says he was wrong about my due date; it's a month later. You can go on the museum project. You'll be back before the baby comes."

Fred had put an arm around her shoulders. "I want to be here to hold your hand. I know it's painful. I was home when my youngest brother was born. My mother screamed. A woman from her church prayer circle came to help. I saw her carry bloody sheets out of my parents' bedroom.

"What shall we name our baby? If it's a boy, maybe Arthur or Robert—my favorite writers are Arthur Conan Doyle and Robert Louis Stevenson. A girl—Constance is a beautiful name."

Genevieve had smiled. "Of course, dear. You're the boss."

A sweet-faced nurse entered Genevieve's hospital room, a cozily wrapped infant cradled in her arms, and laid it beside its mother. "We really recommend bottle-feeding, Mrs. Esmand. Are you sure you want to breast-feed? With two babies, you won't have time for anything else."

"My husband insists."

In reality, Fred had told her he looked forward to cuddling his baby and bottle-feeding it. He told her that after his mother died when he was eight, he'd helped his father care for his two younger brothers, one age four, the other six months. Fred was comfortable with babies.

"This is your first time. I'll show you how. When this baby has finished lunch, I'll bring in her sister."

Genevieve looked down at the sweet-smelling infant. *What ugly babies I have – they look like newborn rats!*

The nurse helped the new mother uncover a breast, showed how to swab her nipple with a cotton ball dipped in warm water, and insert the nipple in the wet little pink mouth that eagerly latched onto it.

Genevieve flinched. *The little bitch bit me!*

"When she's finished, I'll bring in your other daughter."

Oh, shoot! I have to put up with this because I want Fred to watch me nurse the baby and go all goopy. When an artist isn't painting a woman he'd like to make pregnant, he's painting one who's just been pregnant, holding a healthy son in her lap.

Genevieve saw the nurse lingering, staring at her face. People often gazed at her as if at an *objet d'art.*

The art-lover said, "We were worried about you, giving birth to twins when you're so tiny."

At the allusion to her humiliating size, Genevieve firmed her lips. Knowing the nurse was watching, she instantly contemplated her infant with the adoring eyes of a Raphael Madonna. *Why couldn't one be a boy so I could give the Esmands an heir to carry on the family name?* She looked up and smiled at the nurse. *I'll remind them that I'm giving them the first baby in this generation. That'll count for something.*

"I bet your husband and parents are excited. Do your folks live far away?"

"Somewhat." Genevieve evaded such questions. She rarely talked about her family or childhood. She knew many people consider the Amish ignorant, backward peasants because they refuse education past the eighth grade.

Genevieve's parents, Moses and Anna Yoder, were born and reared Old Order Amish, the most conservative sect. Moses' sister had divorced her cruel husband, so the community subjected her to *Bann und Meidung,* Amish excommunication. Almost everyone she had known all her life shunned her as an outcaste. She committed suicide.

Her grieving brother Moses criticized the community for its cruel intolerance, which led to the community putting him under the ban. He left with his wife, Anna, and their five children.

Moses studied agriculture at Purdue and drove a car. He and his wife and children dressed like the "English," the Amish term for everyone not Amish or Mennonite, the more lenient parent sect from which the Amish split in late seventeenth-century Switzerland.

The nurse told her brooding patient, "If a baby's slow to nurse, stroke its cheek, and it'll search for the nipple and start sucking." She chatted pleasantly about her own family until she thought the baby had finished. Laying a clean cloth across Genevieve's shoulder, she showed her patient how, with one hand, to press the baby's tummy against her shoulder, and with the other to rub its back gently until she heard a burp. "Otherwise the baby'll get colicky and cry."

Genevieve smiled at the nurse. *She and Dr. Vorbeck know I had two healthy twins, so Fred must never meet them or come here.*

Bravo

John W. Davis

The Performing Arts as Inspiration for Personal Excellence

Recently I had the privilege of hearing a performance by the San Diego Symphony Orchestra. I marveled at the musicians' skill and resulting beauty that resonated for the audience. As often happens during such a time, my mind wandered back to my recent performance. Not as a musician, but as a whole person.

I was motivated by the talent displayed by these artists to excel in various ways in my own life. Inspiration to give our personal best in all we do. It is another real gift bestowed by the artists. This is a spin off benefit the performing arts give us above and beyond the actual work being performed. I suspect that it is a phenomenon experienced by most, if not all of us.

There is, then, a lot of value in exposing our loved ones, children, and families to artistic performances. Besides helping to discover a new singer, dancer, violinist, or the like, we can help others to be inspired to excellence in their own unique area of interest and expertise.

When we watch a dancer glide effortlessly across the stage, an actor deliver his lines with perfect timing and projection, or a symphony cheer us with a breathtaking rendition of a cherished work, the pleasurable sensation is not only visceral, but also resounds on a subconscious level. The positive influence spills over into our own personal performance in many areas of our lives. Thus, we know it can be a source of positive stimulation for our loved ones and friends, reaping future benefits.

As time passes, we all can get complacent, even sloppy, in how we perform. We all should strive to meet or surpass our own standards of performance. From job performance to cooking and cleaning—almost any area of life you can think of. A great performance can reawaken existing standards or even raise the bar for those who follow.

When we invest time and money in support of our performing arts, it not only gives us the added benefit of enjoyment of the performance, it can have far-reaching effect.

Like the stone skipped across a pond, those benefits can ripple through our lives.

Roommates

Ruth Leyse-Wallace

Fancy a cozy room, if you will,
Where the night is growing still.
You and your 'mate are settling down
In from a day on the road, on the town.

In the comfort of the covers, you're just drifting away,
When the surrounding silence is suddenly at bay.
First a gasp, then a wheeze,
Then suspense when no one breathes;
A gurgle moist then soon evolves
Into a snort that then revolves
And becomes the gasp that starts anew
The cycle that is bathing you.

You toss, you turn, you plug your ears;
Three hours of this and you're in tears.
You concentrate, you meditate,
You contemplate tomorrow's fate.
You can't ignore a sound in the dark;
Your sense of sight is put in "park".
You try so hard to go to sleep,
Trying itself can make you weep.

You read, you rise, you pace the halls,

(At least the sound won't pierce the walls).

Once you're focused, you can't let go,

Though your mind and body want to slow.

That it's "your problem," you accept,

But you don't arise as if you'd slept.

Next to sleep, what would make it right

Is sympathy for your sleepless plight

From someone who knows what you've been through,

Not to be told that you snore too.

The Meeting

Lisa Hunt

From *One Salute Too Many*

Command Information Center (CIC) 0300 hours. It was around 0300 when Chief got up from his Tactical Action Officer watch command seat. He walked over to me at the Digital Dead Reckoning Table. I was on OSP watch (Own Ship Position). This computes and digitally displays latitude/longitude, then plots contacts relative to the ship's position.

Leaning over, he pretended to look at what I was doing. Then, he placed his left hand on my lower back and slid it snakelike down to skim my buttocks, giving them a little tap. He didn't have to say a word. I knew what was on his mind. This had been happening every day for months. My heart clenched in helpless desperation—then dropped into my stomach.

"I'm leaving now to go to TACLOG (the Tactical Logistics room)," he whispered in my ear. "I'll call for you in about ten minutes. I'm going to tell them that I need to discuss your officer package with you."

When he left the room, Campbell, Smith, Vale, Matthews, and Theodore looked over. Theodore sat in the Gunnery Liaison Officer (GLO) position where Matthews sat off watch. I didn't talk to Theodore much, but I could tell by the puzzled look on his face that he was curious about what the Chief had said to me.

Ten minutes later on the dot, Chief called and told Campbell to send me to TACLOG. I didn't want to go, but I didn't know what to say. My reputation was on the line. I understood I was new at the command. I didn't want to create any negative waves. If I said I didn't want to go, I would have been questioned why I wasn't following orders. There was also the thought that if I said anything negative about Chief, he would turn the situation around to make it look as though I were to blame and coming onto him. This was based on a recent experience.

A month before, Chief had written me up for having sex with three Marines on ship. He told me he was jealous and didn't like me talking with males on the ship. He tried to send me to Captain's Mast, which means the commanding officer gets involved and imposes punishment. I refused to sign the counseling chit and wrote a statement agruing against the accusations. Chief's demands were impossible. I had to speak with fellow shipmates every day because I worked with them—most were males.

A couple days later, Chief told me he would drop the accusations. He decided he didn't want to get me in trouble and admitted that he lied out of jealousy. Meanwhile, I was pulled into the Operation Officer's stateroom, where he informed me that I did not have what it takes to be a female officer and was not "honorable." I tried to speak up for myself, but he didn't want to hear anything I had to say. The Operation Officer informed me that although charges were dropped by my Chief, he still considered me "unprofessional."

Becoming a naval officer was my goal and dream. This dishonorable mark on my record was devasting. I saw my future being pulled away beyond my grasp.

Before leaving CIC that morning, Campbell commented about Chief always taking me out of night watch. He told me to tell Chief that I needed to come back right away because of watch stations. Everyone in CIC stared at me as I walked out the door. It was as if they knew what was happening but were afraid to say anything themselves because they didn't want to be caught in the midde of a bad situation.

Opening the office door, I saw him sitting in the same chair as always with an empty chair facing him. He told me to sit down. I obeyed and looked around the room to view any exits other than the door I entered. I thought I was having a panic attack. My heart pounded rapidly. I became lightheaded and disoriented. Sweat drenched the palms of my hands and my body felt like putty. It was as if all four walls were closing in around me.

Grabbing both of my hands, he began to kiss each finger. I tried to pull a hand back, but his hands were twice as large as mine and twice as strong. He leaned into me, violating my personal space. The more his body surrounded me, the more my neck and jaw clenched in fear.

"What are we going to tell our spouses? I don't know how I'm going to tell my wife that I'm leaving her for you. Have you thought about what you're going to tell your husband? What will happen when we get back home? My feelings for you are so strong I don't know if I can hide them much longer. I'm afraid that others on the ship will notice how we feel about each other."

Pulling my hands back onto my lap, I told Chief that I felt uncomfortable and needed to go back on watch. I told him that Campbell needed me for rotation and that I'd been instructed not to be gone for so long. He lifted his hand toward me and began to touch my face, stroking his fingers up and down my right cheek. I could feel my cheeks flame red-hot. I was nervous and tried to gather my thoughts. I knew I had to handle the situation carefully.

"I know you have feelings for me," he said. "You're embarrassed to say it. I understand. I'm afraid to get caught, too."

Leaning into me further, he took both of his hands and placed them around my head. He pulled me forward, his big fat lips puckered to give me a kiss. I leaned my head back and turned my face to the left so that if he kissed anything it would be my ear.

"Stop," I told him.

He stopped for a moment, then he looked at me and said, "I can't help myself. You know, I know how hard you've been working on your officer package. It would be a shame if you didn't get it."

Then he pulled my face toward him and touched me with his

tongue, running it, wet and slimy, along the corner of my mouth. I closed my eyes and held them tight. All I could envision was his tongue on my skin. I didn't want to see his face. Up and down. Up and down, went his tongue. It moved from the top of my lip to the bottom of my lower lip. I jerked back and looked at him with disgust as I wiped off his spit with the sleeve from my coverall. Everything about him revolted me. Just being near him sickened me. I had never before felt such hatred that I would want to physically hurt someone — until that moment.

This was the man I should have seen as a mentor. He was my superior and my boss. He was the same man that gave me the speech on sexual harrassment and how he would not tolerate it. I should be able to trust him, not fear him — not hate him.

Again, I told him that I needed to go back to watch. He said he wanted to look at me a while longer. He said that the others wouldn't be looking for me since they thought I was working on my officer package. Then, he just sat and stared at me. I felt as though time had stopped because I wasn't sure how long I had been sitting in the room. It seemed like an eternity. All I was aware of was how I was a captive with him leering at me, undressing me with his eyes. He didn't speak. The only sound I heard was him — breathing heavily.

Nothing mattered to him. Not my watch. Not my responsibility to duty. None of it mattered. He just wanted me to sit there while he violated his command and destroyed any respect or trust I once had.

Finally, he was done. He told me to get back on watch and to hurry because he didn't want people to start talking. I hurried out into the passageway and ran down to CIC and resumed my watch station, ignoring Campbell's stares. He didn't say anything, but I could tell that he wanted to know what was going on.

What *could* I say? " I just spent two hours like a caged animal locked up with a pervert."

I didn't talk to anyone the rest of watch. I withdrew and kept reliving what Chief had just done to me. Time crawled on. I tried to focus on my job but I was terrified about my future—dreading what might happen next.

Summons

Richard Peterson

Chapter 3

Previously: Chicago detective Roy Dobbs found himself the subject of a space aliens' experiment. The Sat'ka aliens gave him two "gifts": the ability to read minds and to switch into a hyperspeed (physical) mode. Dobbs has "teamed up" with an uber-rich businesswoman, Samantha Crane, to create a new life for himself. However, after dinner with a U.S. senator and a State Department official, the four of them were viciously attacked by assassins in a hotel elevator.

Detective Dobbs locked the front door of his condo and shuffled down the hallway to the living room. He tossed his ruined sports coat onto the leather sofa. The coat had been slashed and two seams ripped by his exertions. Normally that would concern him. But not now. He looked at the sunburst wall clock: 11:35 p.m.

Right now, he needed "egg time"--bad.

Atop one of his bookshelves stood a foot-tall vase, covered with half-inch winding stripes of red, orange, purple, blue, and green. He carefully lifted the vase and placed it on the glass-topped coffee table in front of the leather sofa. Then sat. He wrapped both hands around the middle of the vase. Seconds later a pale yellow light slowly rose from its open top and spread until the light surrounded Dobbs, its curves meeting at a point two feet above his head. He could still hear and see within the "egg;" in fact, during one session he could smell the lentil soup he had simmering on the stove.

The skin of the egg swirled lazily around him like a thin, yellow liquid.

He closed his eyes and leaned back against the sofa cushions. It felt like being submerged in the warm waters of a hot tub. Soon his fatigue, like an unwanted headache, began melting away.

After precisely ten minutes, the egg slowly disappeared, as if evaporating, with only a soft *pfft.* Then a dark blue beam of light leaped from the middle of the vase. The beam, resembling an ultra-thin door, swung back and forth over Dobbs. With each swing it made a *wzzz, wzzz, wzzz....* Somehow this provided communications with the Sat'ka aliens. They had explained that they needed regularly to monitor his thoughts. Also, this was a time when he could pose questions to them. But the Sat'ka were tight-lipped entities. Their answers were always brief and formal; often they provided only a terse statement: "Our ongoing experiment prohibits response."

Puzzling too, they had chosen not to reveal their physical selves. Their communications were always psychic.

His thoughts drifted to Samantha. Tomorrow he'd give his report--in no uncertain terms. He would strongly recommend that she distance herself from Senator Drake.

What the devil did Drake get himself mixed up in? But kidnapping a U.S. senator….

Dobbs couldn't help but marvel at the bravado of such an attempt.

*

He shook his head, remembering. One thing was clear: He needed to polish his martial-arts skills. Tonight's incident proved that.

Since he had been the petite woman's primary target, he had watched as her arms crossed in front of her chest. When her arms whipped back, each fist was tipped with a three-inch-long metal triangle.

As grayish white murk from the smoke pellets surged upward, Dobbs took a quick gulp of air. Held it. He ripped Samantha's handbag from her grasp and swept it around to slam aside one of the sweeping blades. With his right arm he roughly shoved Samantha and Crowley into one corner, then countered more slashing blows from the woman, who grunted and swung her arms at him in precise, measured strokes.

With his second "gift" activated, Dobbs could now move and react up to three times his normal speed. Glancing over, he saw Stocky Man grab and start pushing the senator, as if in slow motion, toward the elevator wall.

Although the killers appeared to be acting as if underwater, they were still deadly, especially the armed woman. The cries and yells from Samantha and Crowley were unnerving.

Ignore, he commanded himself.

Dobbs shouted, "Hey!" to startle the woman, then dropped into a crouch and unfastened the small Glock from his ankle holster. He swiped the barrel at the woman's left leg, but at that level the smoke was thick. He felt only minor impact against her shin. But it brought a shout of pain.

He shifted the Glock for a better grip, but just then someone from behind clawed at his upper arm and the gun was jerked free, clattering onto the floor. *Forget it.* So he plunged a free hand into the handbag.

Coughing — the two women in the corner. *Focus.*

Another grunt. A knife blade grazed his left arm. Angered now, the woman was increasing her efforts, her hands like a whirlwind of stabbing, slashing metal.

There! He yanked out the mini stun gun. Her foot kicked, glancing off his thigh. She shouted and her right hand began coming down, so Dobbs jerked to one side, ripping a coat seam. As he lay on his right side, he strained to see through the smoke.

His lungs were starting to burn.

Come on.

Suddenly a woman's shoe and brown pant leg reared out, almost hitting him in the face. He jabbed the stun gun into her calf. Her legs buckled and she went down.

Gasping, Dobbs pushed himself to his feet. Stocky Man had the senator braced face first against the elevator wall.

Stocky Man barked, *"Schiet op! Schiet op!"* [Hurry up! Hurry up!] so Dobbs stepped over and used a knee against the killer's sacral plexus hard enough to incapacitate, then pulled him out of the way.

*

Dobbs stared at his colorful Jackson Pollock print hanging on the opposite wall. The thin blue beam kept swinging back and forth, *wzzz, wzzz....*

From his mind-scans he knew the killers' intent: to kidnap the senator and leave a bloody message of corpses.

But why? Did this General Cheung have anything to do with it?

Tomorrow at 1 p.m. he would have another question-and-answer session with the FBI. Of course, a big push was on to keep this event from the media. Senator Drake had insisted. Samantha and Tabitha were badly rattled by the incident, but fortunately, only Tabitha sustained minor bruises.

A plus there, he thought. *But kidnapping? Why?*

Dobbs closed his eyes and mentally pushed away the questions. He wasn't getting involved in Drake's business, and yet wouldn't mind seeing the man kicked out of office.

This state deserves better. The blowhard snake...wzzz, wzzz....

Suddenly came a distinct crackling, as if someone were tearing open a cellophane wrapper. He knew instantly: a Sat'ka communication. A human female voice--surprisingly similar to an automated telephone voice--began stating, *Your previous query, as we understand, was, What factors have kept human beings from reaching their full potential? Simply put, ignorance and superstition are two factors. We find it disturbing that your species has stepped foot upon your moon, yet persists in believing in a host of superstitions such as ghosts, the Loch Ness –*

Just then the telephone rang from across the room, its sharp tone jolting. Dobbs' eyes flew open. The Sat'ka voice abruptly stopped. The blue beam froze. Then it soundlessly collapsed into a single, pencil-thin beam, which quickly withdrew back into the middle of the vase.

Dammit! Who the hell – ?

He pushed himself off the sofa and crossed the room, feeling awake and refreshed. Snatched up the handset. Took a few seconds to compose himself. *The FBI?*

"Yes?"

"Detective Dobbs?"

"Yes, it is."

"So sorry to call you at this hour, but it's of utmost importance."

A woman's voice, thick with a cultured British accent.

"Important in what way?" *It better be, the Sat'ka answer....*

"Detective, General Cheung would like to meet with you. Now."

The Watering Hole

Mardie Schroeder

The sun was high overhead. The air was heavy. Both horses stood quietly opposite each other at the watering hole. A drop of water that had escaped one of the horse's mouths was suspended in midair on its downward course to disappear and be enveloped into the pool below--evidence a thirst was quenched, at least for the moment.

One horse was saddled, a canteen tethered to it, a bedroll wrapped in a well-worn slicker tied behind it. The other horse had no saddle, no canteen, no bedroll and no slicker. A thin rope served as a halter and reins.

One man wore jeans, a long-sleeved shirt, worn cowboy boots, a neckerchief, and a hat. The other, younger man, wore a loincloth. His long, lean legs hung relaxed against the flanks of his horse. His feet were enclosed in soft tan moccasins. A white-tipped eagle feather was tucked in the back of his beaded headband. A quiver holding two arrows was slung across his back.

The cowboy had a double-barreled Winchester across his lap. The young brave held his bow on his knee. The notch of the arrow was in the string but remained in a relaxed position.

They regarded each other silently. Neither one of them

appeared as though they wanted a fight. But you never know.

Who would be the first to turn away?

Name On A Rock

Joseph Bonpensiero

There was a time, not too long ago, when the weather and dry air hadn't done its damage to my once young and, I was told, peachy skin. I was just "Julie" then, a country girl from Danville, Illinois. I'm seventy now and in what I like to call my second life. I've lived a life of excitement and joy, sadness, and tragedy—and that's to be expected. Like the song, "I've made mistakes, more than a few...and did it my way."

Now, at peace with myself, I don't look back. Looking ahead is where the living is. I keep young at heart by volunteering as a teacher's aide at an elementary school.

Like an old barnyard hen, I monitor my "chicks," always ready to step in and break up a tussle or assist when they take a tumble or get a scratched knee. Watching over my "brood" of cackling five- and six-year-olds, so full of life and wonder, I am often reminded of raising my own sons and of those very long-ago days, some would say "ancient," when I, too, was just a child.

Those of us of a certain age may find ourselves casting a skeptical eye toward today's teachers and parents. I wonder at the foolishness of an overbooked schedule—enrichment classes or organized sports—do young children need to be so engaged? I wonder. And are all those electronic devices inspiring creativity—

or stifling it?

Perhaps that's why many of the children I see are so starved for simple interaction with adults. How nurturing can it really be if a child spends long periods of time immersed in computers or electronic games?

"Yesterday, I remembered to write a reminder on the chalkboard," I said to a fellow aide during our coffee break.

"The kids asked me what I was doodling. Can you believe they didn't know what cursive writing was?"

We both just shook our heads and added it to the growing list of complaints we share about today's education philosophy.

I couldn't help but wonder if the computer age, for all its wonder and amazing success, was unknowingly placing a stranglehold on free thought. Would "free thought" one day become a thing of the past—all for the sake of expediency and cost-effectiveness?

Yes, the kids of today are taught to rely on computers; but, are they taught how to fall back on their brain when the batteries on those devices die or the plug is pulled from the outlet?

Who, then, I wondered, *or what will run the world?*

I have to wonder in today's "I/me" mentality, with social media keeping track of every move with iPhones and iPads, nano-computers and God knows what else, if anyone is minding the store when it comes to memorizing multiplication tables, spelling words or grammar and punctuation. If this next computerized generation wants to conquer the world, how will they figure out how to get there?

As a senior adult, I might become cynical if it weren't for the occasional little light that sometimes shines bright and renews my faith in humanity. Zoe is one of those little lights.

Yesterday, I had just finished tending to one of my charges who had scraped his knee when Zoe ran up to me, red curly hair flying in all directions, and sporting bright orange tennis shoes with blinding yellow laces and blinking lights. She was excited and couldn't get the words out fast enough.

"What's up, Zoe?"

"Grannie Julie, are you old?"

"Old?" Leave it to kids to strip away the false image and strike at the core of truth.

"Well, some think so," I said laughing. "But, I don't think I'm old. You can feel as old as you want to. Since I hang out with kids like you, I feel pretty young—most of the time."

She studied me for a moment.

"Granny Julie, will my face get wrinkly like yours someday?"

"Hmmm. Well, maybe. You know we are all like an old mop. We've been washing the floor so long that, after awhile, everything starts to frizzle."

"I don't want to get old and wrinkly," Zoe said.

I nodded and we both sat there for a while, watching the other kids at play. Zoe was busy picking at the flowers on her jeans and I was contemplating the certainty of life's unalterable realities.

"Granny Julie, you know what I really want? I want to pass just like my auntie."

I was surprised at Zoe's comment. Young children often say things in the simplest ways and it's always wise to tread lightly. I wasn't sure if she meant "pass" in the sense of "dying" or if it had some other, less-sinister meaning for the child.

"Tell me about your auntie, Zoe."

"I used see my auntie a lot. Then, she got sick. Mom said it was cancer. She said it was 'cause she smoked."

Zoe was swinging her feet back and forth and staring at her shoes. She was quiet. I thought I could almost hear the little wheels in her head humming. Then, she looked at me with all the sparkle of pure unadorned, unbiased, innocence.

"I used to visit her. She made peanut-butter and jelly sandwiches. She cut them in shapes like hearts. Sometimes, we'd work in the garden. We loved flowers. We used to plant them and water them and when they grew up, they had babies."

I thought this seemed like a safe segue.

"How nice that you did that with your auntie, Zoe. Flowers are such friendly things, aren't they.

Zoe had gone back to studying her shoes.

"Yep. You know what, Grannie Julie? Now, auntie has her own garden on a hill with grass all around. She moved to a new place. Mommy called it a sem-e-tary."

I nodded solemnly.

"And, you know what? My auntie had a peach-colored bed, all silky. That's where she's sleeps now."

"That's nice, isn't it?" I said.

"Yeah." Zoe was picking at the flowers on her jeans, again. "She was my favorite, you know."

"I would guess so."

"And you know what else? They put her name on a rock. That's so I can find where she's sleeping. Can you believe that, when you go to sleep like that they put your name on a rock."

Zoe seemed to be at peace with her story. I nodded, agreeing with her.

"You must sure miss your auntie."

"Not really," replied Zoe. "She's sleeping in a beautiful bed. She has her flowers and a new address so I know where to find her."

Zoe saw her friends and scampered off.

I couldn't help wonder at Zoe's wise acceptance of

death. She had simplified the truth by creating a safe harbor to understand the loss of her precious aunt. With pure, child-like wisdom, little Zoe had created an uncomplicated answer to one of life's most perplexing questions. There was no long-winded discussion about esoteric existence and issues of death and dying. Zoe didn't need a complicated discussion about whether her auntie was in heaven or someplace else. Zoe had no doubt that everything was as it should be.

For Zoe, everything was okay. Her auntie had a beautiful new bed, a new address—and her name on a rock.

In the end, it all comes down to that.

It's Never Too Late

Amy E. Zajac

My eldest daughter flourished in junior high school. However, shortly after that, teenage issues introduced a new defiance into our day-to-day life. Discipline became difficult when she fought for independence as unforeseen events challenged her to learn how to choose direction.

Over the next couple of years, her independent thought led to ditching classes. It alarmed me that she skipped with no regret.

Daily communication from the high school office complicated our lives. I explained how truancy jeopardized her grades and her participation in drill team. To complicate matters, her dad thought talking to her was unnecessary because her opinion didn't matter. He believed in discipline only.

My husband and I disagreed fiercely. Arguments ignited. Understanding why, from my point of view, would allow for the correct punishment. She could learn to make better decisions sooner if we listened to the reasons for her actions.

During the turmoil of daily family life, her younger sister was diagnosed with cancer when she discovered a lump on her leg. It was shortly after that, during a confrontation, that my older daughter's life turned upside down over an absurd argument. Unable to deal with a young, logical thinker, her dad removed her from our home.

I was torn up by the incident. No matter what I did I would disrupt our family. My child needed me. I found a temporary place for her to live. With our current family situation, I already planned to leave my marriage.

A key part of my moving day involved bringing her home to again live with her sister and me. Once my friends and I moved my belongings into the new apartment, I went to pick her up.

Although I wanted to have her back with us, her month of total freedom promoted living in a non-restrictive environment. She virtually did anything she wanted.

While she lived away from home, she passed her driving test. I was overjoyed. I managed to get a second car. She found a job close by because she needed to pay for car insurance. I relied on her to help me with driving. This freed me to manage the delicate balancing act of working while handling her sister's health needs.

Her responsible driving gave me hope and made me proud. She appeared to be reliable, so I trusted her to drive to meet me for dinner, to her grandparent's house, and to church. But this dependability contrasted with other parts of her life.

I hoped her school attendance would improve; however, it deteriorated. The high school notified me that non-attendance now turned into failure and she would no longer be able to attend the city high school. They set her up at the technical school across town that dealt with troubled students.

I tried to talk to her. Anger and pain showed on her face and her flip attitude deepened our friction. It embarrassed her to attend the technical school. Her grades were always good, even though she rarely studied. Her problem was attendance.

These two very mixed up and different life traumas required me to delicately adjust the scales with my attention. Both my daughters needed me. One to support her life-threatening illness and the other to support her deteriorated life due to poor school-related decisions, complicated further by controversial family situations.

The weekend before starting the new school, she took off with friends, walking in the door just after 2:00 a.m. Her trite accounting of the time: she "skied until midnight, after that, visited with friends."

Since we still hadn't talked about what this new school meant, I drove the first day so we could talk on the way. At school, I parked in the back row. I turned off the engine; the deafening silence hung between us. I twisted in my seat to face her and took a deep breath. What I was about to say to her broke my heart. She looked so young, sad, and lonely.

"Okay, here you are. I know this is the last place you want to be, but the choices you made to skip classes brought you here. You're at a decision point. What you do from now on basically decides who you will be in the future. You can choose to succeed here at this school. You're the only person who can do this. I can't get you out of it. Plus, with all that's going on with your sister, I won't be able to hold your hand through it all. I'll support you no matter how you decide to handle what's in store for you, but you'll have to do it on your own. You can do whatever you want with your life."

She nodded. "I understand."

We hugged each other a long time before we walked into her new school together.

The school offered a program that allowed her to work at her own pace. Fast. She worked with a fury through many lunch hours and exceeded the program's criteria every week. To complete the program so she could get back to the city high school drove her. Through the grapevine, we learned it was unlikely she would be able to go back to her old school. "It's never been done before." She needed to complete multiple programs successfully with good grades, plus both principals needed to approve. She knew all this and kept working the programs anyway, talking daily about friends and graduation.

Months went by, and although she kept telling me how much work she accomplished at school, I really didn't expect what happened next. The principal of the technical high school called me. She explained that my daughter had completed all the program sets required and qualified to apply for readmission to the city high school. The technical high school principal recommended to the city high school principal that she be readmitted because not only was her attendance perfect, but she also completed her multiple programs in record time. No one had ever completed all the school requirements in such a short period.

I signed the completed application and so did the technical high school principal, who wrote a glowing review.

The call came from the city high school indicating that she would be readmitted as of the next Monday.

At this notification, my daughter bounced off the walls. She would graduate with her original class once she completed some extra credit. Her excitement and enthusiasm were contagious!

Through her actions, she showed it's never too late to change direction and her new option proved powerful. Turning all the "errors in judgment" into a personal success story became a model throughout her adult life, tackling her collegiate education and multiple long-distance moves while working in the educational industry.

No matter what challenge she encountered, she confronted it head-on, including the day she walked in the door and said, "Mom, I've been accepted into the Los Angeles Sheriff's Academy!"

Talking To You

R. J. Black

Talking to you
is like calling at dolphins
to come out and play on the beach.
I turn blue in the face.

Talking to you
is like calling the plays from the sofa
as the Packers play the Chargers on TV.
I turn blue in the face.

Talking to you
is like telling my shadow
to stop following me.
I turn blue in the face.

Talking to you
is like praying to God
to re-grow an amputated leg.
I turn blue in the face.

Talking to you

is like ... talking to you

is like ... talking to you.

I turn blue in the face.

Words and Music

John Cain

From *Gig Tales*

Waxing philosophical — that unsightly wax buildup.

Buried in the bottom lines of a recent e-mail chat with writer John Wolf, he wrote this:

"We are of what we can understand and we only understand what our words can tell us. Twenty-six letters like the twelve-tone scale is an endless canvas to express our tales, climb over walls of controversy, conquer countries with sweeping verbosity, or be lost in hollow accounts of what we cannot think when at a loss for words."

His words, as a professional musician, really struck a chord with me, so to speak, because I'm a musician who wrote a book about music and musicians, rather than a writer who wrote a book about music.

As a musician I'm accustomed to expressing myself with music, but in writing a book it was a difficult challenge for me to do so with words. So, Wolf's words got me thinking about the correlations between the written word and music. Though both of these genres of expression require talent and practice of craft, I believe it is more difficult to express moods and emotions with words than with music. Let me explain.

Written words and music have a couple of things in common: a piece of writing, an essay, a poem, short story or novel can be considered the equivalent to the musical performance of a composer's work. Also, the effect of the writer's work and the composer's tune is internal. It happens within the mind of the reader and the listener. A major difference, however, is that a writer creates his work in private whereas a musician creates his work in public.

When you perform live music the reward is instant because the performance and the audience are present in the moment. (Or you can bomb in an instant, too!) Writing is more of a vicarious marathon. An author doesn't get instant feedback. The book goes out there and he hopes people read it and like it, but he's not there to know what their reaction is to his work. It takes time for that to happen.

This subject of music as language is the topic of endless discussion among musicians. Music, we have decided, actually has a larger lexicon than spoken or written language even though it uses merely 12 tones. But because music is sound, it is more akin to spoken language than written language. In a few seconds music can communicate moods, feelings and imply ideas that would require hundreds of words to express in writing and much more time for the reader to understand. With writing, things must be described, defined and explained.

As human creatures we are full of imagination, ideas,

fantasies and emotions that if we were to speak about in normal everyday life with others, they'd throw a net over us. It is considered inappropriate to discuss certain things, especially fantasies, in public. But it is acceptable to express them with music and other forms of art.

Since communication is a two-way street the recipient of music, the listener, is in on the game. The music says what the listener is feeling or wants to say but can't because he is, as Wolf says, "…lost in hollow accounts of what we cannot think when at a loss for words." On some subliminal level he or she understands the meaning of what the music is saying. The listener "gets it." The music is expressing something the listener has felt but could never put into words exactly.

A writer, on the other hand, does put it into words exactly. Using 26 letters of the alphabet the writer's skill is to literally express those same taboo ideas and feelings with words, and to do this without having someone throw a net over him or getting thrown in jail. And, of course this happens to writers all too often. Do we need a reminder of how important freedom of speech is?

Written words are usually deemed more dangerous than musical expression. Writers who broach taboo subjects or tell the naked truth are always getting into trouble with the authorities, particularly when they critique those in power or whip up a revolution. (American revolutionary troublemaker Thomas Paine comes to mind.)

Good composers of music really know how to yank one's emotional chain in the same way a good writer can tell a story that will bring a tear to one's eye or make the reader laugh out loud.

About 350 years ago, Johann Sebastian Bach figured it all out, at least for the musical lexicon. He made a list of all the major and minor keys and assigned emotional values to each key (the key of D-minor being the saddest key of all).

Music also has the unfair advantage of using the timbre of the musical instruments. These are like the voices of the characters in a novel. For example, a composer knows that the timbre of a tuba can sound like a fat guy and the trilling of a flute can sound like a ballerina. How about the famous John Williams score for the movie *Jaws?* Ever since, the sound of bass fiddles bowing in unison that simple half-step interval, *(low-high…low-high…duh-duh…duh-duh),* makes us think of a huge great white shark about to attack.

One of the smallest instruments is the harmonica yet its timbre seems to wield extraordinary emotional impact on the listener, particularly in American culture. The harmonica evokes images of a lonely railroad track, the blues of a destitute prisoner, or it can be happy like a country hoedown, or draw images of the immensity of the open prairies and the Wild West.

Then there are the more comic musical sounds; banjoes and kazoos go together to make a silly mood, so do a slide whistle with a pie in the face or a bicycle horn with a rubber chicken. A slide trombone with marimba and ocarina together will express lighthearted whimsy. And what would a Borscht Belt comedian be without his punch-line rim shots?

A writer, on the other hand, has to use words to imply or describe what the voice of the characters sounds like so that the reader imagines the sound in his mind. A skillful writer can weave his tale with words, evoking a sense of mystery, terror, irony or humor without all the advantages of musical instruments.

The writer's task is to communicate without the advantage of sound. His talent is to tell a story, evoke moods, inform and hypnotize, to create a world inside the mind of the reader with nothing but words. And what power these words have when wielded by a skillful writer. Just as Wolf said, with words we…"climb over walls of controversy, conquer countries with sweeping verbosity."

Words and music are the sacred language of our species and we have the right to use them as we choose. But the power of music and words can be used for good or evil.

Written words and pieces of music can and have been used to both inspire and brainwash. People have laughed, cried, fallen in love, been imprisoned and killed for music and words.

So, just like comic book superheroes, let's vow to use our powers as writers and musicians for good, not evil!

Life's Lessons

Marie DiMercurio

My journey started when I reached a crossroads of life. I felt like I wanted to jump off the face of the earth when things got tough and addictions were getting the best of me. I had gone through many addictions and withdrawals—all painful journeys of recovery, and I could not go there again. I had spent the better part of my life yo-yo dieting, suffering with bulimia and anorexia, and finally realized that I would not be fat if I had never dieted in the first place. I finally realized that I could not do a single thing by myself to change myself, my life, my body, or the situations of my existence. I admitted I am truly powerless—powerless over alcohol, caffeine, refined sugars and flours, preservatives, additives, processed foods/fast foods, junk foods, all chemicals, all drugs.

One can let go of the other addictions, but what about food? I have struggled over the years with my passion to eat. We don't stop eating; after all, food is what sustains our body and our lives. I ask myself, "Do I want caffeine, refined sugars and flours, preservatives, additives, processed foods/fast foods, junk foods, in my life? Do I really *need* these things in my life?"

For my body and me to function optimally, I say "no" to both of those questions. I am powerless over the effects that they have on me. I have learned to compromise throughout the years to fulfill a "craving" for food or drink. Now, I make my own foods without any chemicals, using ingredients that my body can handle.

The process is continuous; the cravings (which are the tip of the iceberg) will come. So it has become another one of life's lessons. It takes pulling away from the table to learn what satiated is. It is a silent emotional struggle; a dialogue between my body and me. Another of life's lessons was to listen to my body. The rule of the body is not to overeat. There is a fine line between being satisfied and feeling full. Many others just know it; they eat until they are satisfied, but as a food addict, I had to learn it. Even if it tastes good, I can't keep on eating until it's gone. I only have two choices, sickness or health.

The only way I've gotten through the last 32 years of my life was taking that first step through the doors of Alcoholics Anonymous (A.A.) and looking at life from the bottom up—using the Twelve Steps of A.A., starting at Step 1: Admit that I am powerless over alcohol and other addictive behavior and that my life has become unmanageable.

What I learned is to be *gut-level honest* with myself and with God—to admit that I'm vulnerable. And I had learn to like myself, as well as to love myself, as God loves me. When I learned that, I did not want to continue to destroy my body any longer. I learned to respect and cherish the one and only me, to take responsibility for myself. To be a victim no longer.

Through this course of learning, I am gaining freedom and peace of mind. I have learned never to look back with any longing for anything, but to look forward to a new life, one *moment* at a time.

God grant me the serenity to accept the things I cannot change,
courage to change the things I can,
and the wisdom to know the difference.

(The Serenity Prayer)

Jerome's Serenade

Carolyn Jaynes

My Sunday afternoon skate at Mission Beach turned into naptime. I parked my car facing the sea to feel the warm western sun on my face and breathe the fresh ocean air. Instead of snoozing, I felt the twinge of holiday distance between me and my out-of-state family, so I called my aunt to wish her a Merry Christmas. Relaxing, I leaned back into my cozy leather-lined Jaguar to have a conversation.

Then I noticed an attractive older man at a picnic table with his guitar. As a professional singer, I wondered if he would know any of my songs, or if I'd know his? I watched as he packed up his music and walked to his vintage van. He looked over at me on my cell phone, then put his guitar inside and disappeared behind the cargo door.

Was he leaving before we could make music together? I hoped he wasn't leaving. Why was I drawn to him? I felt like taking a risk to go talk to him, but maybe it was too late now.

Then he stood there, looking at me, like he felt my vibe. I nodded and smiled to encourage him. He took a step closer. I welcomed him with a thumbs-up. I was still on the phone with my aunt. He pointed to my sparkly Christmas necklace I wore of red, green, and silver and nodded with approval. I laughed and shook the beads to flaunt them. He walked over to my open car window. I ended my call. Standing close to me, he showed me his glossy concert poster.

"I'm Jerome. I'm a musician," he beamed as he pointed to the handsome lead guitarist in the photo.

I was impressed. "I'm a singer." Instant rapport.

"Would you like me to play for you?" he said, grinning.

"Yes, I'd like that." Delighted, I stepped out of my car and met him at the picnic table, where he brought his guitar. He strummed slowly. I hummed along. His composition was original—the work of a genius. Mesmerized by his lyrics, I heard how he felt, how he viewed things. He seemed kind and sentimental. My ears felt gently caressed by his skillful hands, his unique tune vibrated inside my awakening heart. No one else stopped to listen. Was I the only one receptive enough to hear it?

The beach was sparsely attended, except for a few hungry seagulls—his feathered fans fed by his music fare. I, too, was being nourished by his notes. My soul stirred as I watched his long black fingers strum his strings. Spellbound, entranced by his magic, I sat as safe as a drowsy kitten in her owner's lap, yet my body was four feet away from his—respectfully spaced on the picnic bench facing the western skyline, overlooking the sea. His music felt familiar and yet—weren't we strangers?

"I feel like I know you," he said after he sang his original love song which I could have co-written. I knew exactly what he meant. Our comfort together was too good to be a chance meeting. Had we known each other in another life?

Tapping my red sandals to his beat, I interjected my sparse but spicy lyrics to his blues bars. I closed my eyes and took in his unique sound. I praised each song — wanting more. We spent the afternoon this way, timeless, in slow motion. There was no place else I wanted to be. I merged into his sensual serenade. He with his manly New York voice, harmonizing with my girlish Minnesota accent. My eyes studied his thick, sexy lips. Later I learned he had studied mine. Who is he? Him, black as ebony, me, so white.

"I love your skin," he said.

"I love your music." I applauded.

Then a spectacular sunset, right on cue, made its grand finale to his extraordinary concert. Silently, we both watched the pink-orange horizon, transfixed. Nearly breathless, I felt a large tear drop onto my cheek as the sea swallowed the sun.

Jerome turned to me softly, "There's only one first time."

It sounded so sweet. He was right. This was it — a profound meeting of two souls.

"It's time for me to go." It was dark and I had a speaking engagement. If I didn't leave now, I'd be late.

"I wish I could go with you," he shared.

Our hearts had connected. His music was the bonding bridge for two lonely artists at Christmastime. After several hours, it was time to separate from an intimacy that could not have been more perfect if planned. Yet none of it was. Or was it?

I returned his jacket, which smelled like designer cologne, and his warm blanket that he thoughtfully provided to shield me from the wind. "Thank you for a lovely afternoon." I hugged him goodbye. As we parted I felt like a lotus flower, my heart had blossomed from his tenderness. I drove away from him knowing I'd never be the same.

Young Love and Agriculture

Wayne Williams

The farmer's daughter

Gave me a glance

My heart melted.

Jumping off the hay bales in the barn loft together

Gave me more chances.

I could see the outline

Of her panties through her jeans

And the smooth round white of her breasts

Through her sleeveless blouse.

That was fifty-five years ago.

I'm still longing for another glance:

My heart remains melted

Thinking about that country lass.

I wrote to her for twenty years

Baited prose replete with innocent youth.

My life is better for having

Loaded that hay in the barn

In the first place and writing all those letters.

The last time I saw her in Minneapolis
She gave me a kiss as we said goodbye
I wanted to steal her away
From her husband and daughter
And make some more hay.

Civilization wouldn't permit that
Even on the farm in the secret
Hayloft of youth.
Besides, I would have broken her
Innocent heart with my vulgarity.

Now she remains as fine thoughts
Somewhere up in northern Minnesota
Even eons pass quickly.

Owls

Lawrence Carleton

On the fourteenth of May, Daphne woke up late. She wanted
to sleep in even later, but a high-pitched trill outside her bedroom
window lured her into consciousness. She struggled out of bed
and trudged over to open the blinds. She looked out, and
discovered a screech owl perched in the apple tree and staring
right at her.

"Owls again," she muttered, studying the bird. "Owls in the
daylight." Then she thought, "Maybe it's sick. If it's still there at
lunchtime, I should call animal control."

A month before, there'd been an infestation of barn owls. At
first people had associated that with the unexplained rumbling,
"like an earthquake but you don't have those in Michigan," from
the previous day. Then people noticed kids getting sick, pets and
then some elderly neighbors dying in homes outside of which the
owls had perched for several days. Actually, precisely seven days
was the key duration. Friends and neighbors panicked.

Old Piers Hamlyn seized the opportunity: he proposed, for a
fee, to lure the owls from the neighborhood to his woodlot miles
out of town. On the big day, Daphne heard Old Piers' ice cream
truck rolling along the street past her house, then up and down
connected streets playing something more resembling a scream

than the usual Pop Goes the Weasel jingle, and she watched the owls flocking and spinning silently around the truck as it made its way.

"Pied Piper Piers," they called him. Superstitions had been reinforced when the news spread that the day after Piers had lured the owls to a pond in his remote woodlot, sixteen fish and two turtles had been found dead in the suddenly still pond. At least the owls had disappeared.

Yesterday there'd been another rumbling in the earth, and now here was this screech owl. Daphne phoned Al. Daphne had been allowed to work from home during the last weeks of her pregnancy. The baby was due the twenty-first. Al hadn't been that lucky. He still had to get up early and drive to work — sometimes in Traverse City, usually at the field station. At least he always set out the makings of breakfast before he left. He didn't wake her. She phoned him when she was up and ready to start work.

"Screech owl, you say?" Al answered her when she described the situation. "Maybe it's your mother come back to watch over the birth of her grandchild." He thought he was funny. "Anyway, have you asked around? Is it another infestation?"

Daphne hadn't thought of that.

It turned out that several neighbors did find owls newly watching them. "Time to call up Piers the Piper again," more than one neighbor proposed.

Daphne was disappointed this time as before in her otherwise intelligent friends' superstition. "What about the earthquakes just before the owls show up?" At most, to her friends, that was just part of the manifestation, not a possible explanation, say, that the birds had been dislodged and disoriented by some event in their usual haunts.

Al should have been in a position to know about the rumblings, given his government job. The best he could offer, though, was a guess. "The natural gas operations, maybe. They could be doing horizontal fracking now: high-pressure water laced with a witches' brew of chemicals, forced underground for miles to break up formations and release natural gas — and still more chemicals. But they don't have to tell us when or even if they're doing it. I've put in some calls, and they're not telling. Boss said stop asking. By the way," he lowered his voice, "don't panic, but I think I'd better bring home some bottled water and some stuff to take samples of our tap water. Don't let on for now."

Al's hunch about the water had been right. Greenwood had to close down its main well and request rationing while it relied on subsidiary sources. Meanwhile, "Momma Owl" was to be found on her perch outside the bedroom window every day when Daphne woke up.

Around noon on the eighteenth of May, Daphne thought she heard gunshots, and, looking out the kitchen window, realized there was a small hole in it. Stepping out to the backyard she noticed several other small holes in the wall around the window.

"Stand back!" yelled Mark Bentley, cocking his weapon. "I'll rid you of that menace if I get a clean shot."

"You'll do no such thing," declared Daphne, surprising herself, given her condition, as she marched to the apple tree to position herself between owl and marksman. "You remove yourself from my property and don't come back unless you bring a dead mouse for Momma Owl's dinner."

"Just doing you a favor," Bentley apologized as he let himself out through the gate. "You know what happens after seven days."

The owl turned her head to follow Daphne's movements. "I guess we have to watch out for each other, don't we?" she whispered. She studied the owl's face. Did it understand?

The twentieth was a Sunday, which was good because Daphne's water broke and Al had to pack her into the car and rush her to Traverse City. They had to wait in the driveway as Piers Hamlyn's ice cream truck rolled slowly past their house, playing its owl music and attracting another swirling collection of softly flapping birds. "Turn left!" Daphne ordered. The shorter route was to the right but she didn't want to follow Piers' truck.

They got home after dark on the twenty-first, tucking their new baby into the bassinet next to their own bed.

In the morning, just at daylight, Daphne awoke to the familiar trilling outside the bedroom window. She opened the blind. The screech owl stared in from her perch in the apple tree, bobbed up and down seven times, and silently flew off.

The Greatest Power in the Universe

Ruth Leyse-Wallace

Don't you just love to have friends to sit around with, drink coffee, philosophize and talk, talk, talk?

When I lived in Topeka, Kansas I had a friend like that. He talked nutrition like I talk nutrition, but he also wrote, published, marketed and sold nutrition booklets. Our favorite philosophical conversation consisted of my trying to convince him that love is the greatest power in the universe, with Bob playing the devil's advocate, countering my ideas with a scientific fact or conjecture leading another direction. We had our discussions at odd hours so we could stretch a pot of coffee without making the waitresses at Denny's too impatient.

After a few years I moved away from Topeka and we didn't keep in touch, not by letter or by telephone. One night, 20-plus years later, and living in Tucson, Arizona, I had one of those crystal-clear dreams with color, sound, and feelings. In the dream I saw Bob coming down the sidewalk and went to greet him. It was a joyful time! We picked up the conversation right where we had left off, and walked together down the street to a McDonald's. We went into the inflated play area where kids jump and joined them—jumping around, laughing, and having such a lot of fun! After a few minutes, we sat down on the plastic bubbles. Bob looked right at me and said, "I just came to tell you that you were right," and … "poof," I woke up.

It was so unusual that the next morning I searched around, found his old number, and called Bob, wondering if he still lived at the same place after twenty years. It was his voice on the answering machine, but he didn't pick up, so I left a message and my new telephone number so he could call me back and hear about the dream.

That evening I got a call from Bob's son. "You must be psychic," he said. "My Dad died last night."

Reflections on Re-tire-ment

Simone Arias

Finally figured out re-tire-ment —
Rubber once worn bare
Now retread for journey ahead.

Endless stretches entice.
Peregrination solely for fascination.
Rambling, careening, sauntering
Mile by mile, coast to coast.

Reflecting in rain,
Racing in rays,
Fading memories of days that daze.

Maps unmapped to unchart the course,
Celebrating serendipity, bound beyond bends.
Leisurely pace transforms the face,
Aging without disgrace.

Traveling Through Transnistria

Sandra Yeaman

When the former Soviet Union broke apart in 1992, Transnistria, a sliver of land stuck between Moldova and the Ukraine, wanted to be part of Russia, not Moldova. Transnistria continued to use the Russian ruble even after Russia had stopped accepting the old-style currency as legal tender. The Transnistrians added a postage stamp to the Russian rubles to indicate they were *their* currency.

Since the collapse of the Soviet Union, Russian troops have been present in Transnistria. At the time my husband, Alex, and I were in Moldova, General Alexander Lebed was in command of the Russian 14th Guards Army in Moldova. Border skirmishes were frequent between Moldova and Transnistria. However, travel across the border was common and somewhat safe. So we were delighted when we were invited to participate in one such trans-border excursion.

The Organization for Security and Cooperation in Europe (OSCE), charged with facilitating a negotiated settlement between Moldova and Transnistria, has had a presence in Moldova since the early 1990s. While we were in Moldova, the ambassador from the OSCE to Moldova was a Canadian. One weekend, he, his wife, Oksana (one of his local staff), the U.S. Ambassador to Moldova

Mary Pendleton, Alex, and I set off for a relaxing few days in Odessa, on the Black Sea coast of the Ukraine.

Ambassador Pendleton had one condition for this trip — that we must cross Transnistria during daylight. She agreed to the OSCE ambassador's plan with the understanding that we return from Odessa in plenty of time to reach the border by 5 p.m.

We left Friday afternoon in two cars. Ambassador Pendleton, Alex, and I were in one car. The OSCE ambassador, his wife and Oksana were in the lead car so Oksana could translate. She was to explain to the guards at the Transnistrian "border," recognized by neither the U.S. government nor most European nations, why we needed to be given speedy and unimpeded passage through Transnistria to the Ukraine.

Oksana had been a university student in Odessa and very eager to show us what Odessa had to offer. Getting us through the Transnistrian checkpoint was not a problem, she assured us. And, just as promised, at the border, Ambassador Pendleton was waved through without having to stop.

Once we reached Odessa, we checked in at a private sanitarium at the edge of the city. The name conjured up visions of patients with tuberculosis or schizophrenia, but Oksana explained that the sanitarium had converted its rooms to accommodate travelers and was a place that offered a relaxing and calming setting. We were the only guests that weekend.

That evening we ate at a restaurant overlooking the coastline and beach. We found the usual on the menu: pelmeni (meat-stuffed dumplings smothered in sour cream), cabbage rolls (meat-stuffed cabbage leaves smothered in sour cream), carrot and raisin salad (smothered in sour cream), and pork. The restaurant was full of very well-dressed, cosmopolitan young couples, some of whom looked as though they had just walked out of a stylish European casino. They were the local "businessmen" who had quickly figured out how to make money in the new capitalist economies of the Commonwealth of Independent States (CIS), the loose confederation of the former Soviet republics.

The next day we toured several museums. We also saw the Potemkin steps, originally 200 steps leading from the city situated on a high steppe plateau to the harbor. The steps are now known more for Sergei Eisenstein's use of them in his 1925 silent film, *Battleship Potemkin*, about the 1905 massacre of sailors and city residents.

That evening we went to a concert, where one of the most noticeable acknowledgements of the change in the government was the hole in the flag on the stage curtain where the hammer and sickle had been.

After the concert, Oksana suggested we go to a hotel that was well known for its entertainment. As she had done at nearly every other stop, she chose that we not park directly in front of the location where we intended to spend our time. Instead, she had the OSCE ambassador drive around the corner from the hotel, where she located two parking spots so that the two cars would be parked one in front of the other. We didn't ask why we didn't park in front of the location; we just wondered. We should have asked; we didn't realize why until later.

The next morning, Sunday, and our last day in Odessa, Oksana recommended we have breakfast at a famous downtown restaurant, Varadero, which offered tables along the open windows overlooking the wide veranda, before we headed a short distance out of town to see another Ukrainian Black Sea site.

Although there were plenty of parking spaces directly in front of the restaurant on a very wide sidewalk where others parked their cars, Oksana again took us around the corner to park the two cars out of sight.

At the end of the meal, as we turned the corner to get back to the cars, we saw immediately that something was wrong. There was only one car on the street, Ambassador Pendleton's Honda. The OSCE ambassador's Lada was missing.

Instead of spending a short time at the other resort, after which we planned to travel back through Transnistria, arriving at the border while it was still daylight—we ended up back at the restaurant where Oksana called the police.

Gasoline was in very short supply in all of the former Soviet Union at that time. After speaking with the police, Oksana informed us that if we wanted someone to investigate the missing car, we would have to pick up a policeman in our remaining car.

The police had no gasoline.

Ambassador Pendleton, the OSCE ambassador, and Oksana headed out to the police station to do that, leaving the OSCE ambassador's wife, Alex, and me behind.

Once the policeman was on site, he seemed optimistic that the ambassador's car would be found. He recommended that we just wait. In the meantime, Ambassador Pendleton, the OSCE ambassador, and Oksana drove the policeman around, making several other stops so he could file the reports and investigate options.

By 3 p.m., Ambassador Pendleton was concerned that if we didn't leave soon, we would arrive at the Transnistrian border at dusk.

"We need to leave," she said. "Now!"

"Don't worry," reassured Oksana. "I know a shortcut that will get us to the border quickly. We don't have to rush yet. Let's wait to see if the police can find the car. Besides, there are six of us. We can't all fit into one car."

"We can squeeze four people in the back seat," countered the ambassador. "It won't be comfortable, but it will be safe."

"The policeman is sure they will find the car soon," insisted Oksana.

We gave in and agreed to wait. By 5 p.m., Ambassador Pendleton had had enough.

"We can't wait any longer," insisted the ambassador. "We

must leave, now!"

"If you must,"replied Oksana. "The OSCE ambassador and I will remain here until the police find the car."

With that, the four of — Ambassador Pendleton, Mrs. OSCE Ambassador, Alex and I — now minus the only Russian speaker among us, headed for the border, taking the shortcut Oksana recommended as the sun sank lower and lower. By the time we reached the border, daylight was nearly gone and we realized that we might have trouble. The guards were not in identifiable uniforms. Most of them were very young men, and it was clear that they had been drinking all afternoon.

When the car stopped, a guard stumbled as he walked towards the car. His rifle was slung over his shoulder while the other guards were holding their rifles by the barrels, resting the butts on the ground, like walking sticks. This behavior did not instill confidence.

The Ambassador rolled down the window and showed him her passport. We sat back, trying not to convey our nervousness.

The guard insisted the ambassador get out of the car. She tried to speak with him in Romanian. Ignoring that attempt, he motioned for her to go to the back of the car and he pointed to the trunk, indicating she should open it. She did. But when he started opening the suitcases in the trunk, she pushed his hands out of the way and told him — in English, which he clearly didn't understand — that he didn't have any right to inspect anything in her car because we were all diplomats and her car had diplomatic plates on it.

In a show of absolute bravado, she slammed the trunk shut, got back into the car, put it in gear and drove off. The rest of us, expecting the worst, slunk down into the seats so our heads were below the level of the back window.

It took a few minutes before we all exhaled.

The OSCE ambassador's car was never recovered.

Ouch!

Ken Yaros

"Dixie, get away, girl! Go on! Let me sleep!"

Josh pushed Dixie, their three-year-old golden Labradoodle, away, but not before she managed to slather him with a few wake-up kisses before hopping down from the bed.

Josh buried himself further under the crazy-patchwork quilt, a family heirloom that his wife Laura's great-grandmother sewed almost eighty years ago. Today of all days he needed its warmth and security. He reached for Laura. "Good morning, honey," he whispered.

"Shush," she mumbled. "Just give me five more minutes before the kids wake up."

*

"Okay, you kids!" Laura shouted down the hall. "It's time for breakfast—you have three minutes; I'm counting!"

Nine-year-olds Michael and Nancy were down in a flash. Nancy, always prompt, had showered and already brushed her teeth. Michael, the procrastinator, had waited until morning to finish his homework on his bed. Petite Aime, aged six, was the biggest challenge.

"I don't want to go to school today, look how cold it is, *please Mommy!*" she whined, then plopped her little frame in the chair at her place at the kitchen table.

Laura dished out hearty bowls of oatmeal, with hot toast and a pot of homemade jelly, grateful that her little brood wasn't picky eaters.

*

Josh finished up in the shower. He picked up his dress shirt and was about to slip on his tie when he hesitated. Perhaps it was the cheerful colors of the quilt that made him reflect on the good things in his life: Laura, the kids, even their bed — a surprise wedding gift from Laura's mom. The huge four-poster king with hand-carved pineapple ornaments at the apex of each post was a subtle yet obvious symbol of family and their comfortable middle-class lives.

Josh glanced at the framed photo on the nightstand — their wedding picture. He wondered how different his life would have been had he attended law school in Hartford, near his family, as he had intended, instead of the small private school in upper-state New Hampshire. *I wouldn't have met Laura*, he thought, smiling.

Becoming an attorney was what he had wanted since junior high school. As it turned out, going away to school was fine with his mom and dad. Sam, Josh's dad, a physician, thought the away-experience would be broadening; Julia, his mom, still had two other children at home to mentor.

Funny how things always seem to work out for the best, he thought, wondering if that would always be true.

*

Josh backed his new Volvo wagon out of the garage. He really could not afford it, but he couldn't chance being seen in a faded older car rusting from road salt either. That definitely would not be the successful attorney image. And *image* is everything today.

And speaking of image, it was a good thing that most clients would never have to see his dingy two-room office, which rented for only $350 a month with its solitary rain-spattered window, sans closet or a private bathroom. He was fortunate enough to have been able to afford a part-time secretary. Still, it was better than the alternative, being in a high-stress job he once had with a prestigious firm in New York City.

When he graduated from law school, there were no jobs to be found. Like many aspiring lawyers, he moved to "the Big Apple" for the experience and for the pay. It was his worst nightmare.

The position promised a six-figure income, private workspace with secretary and a five-day week. However, within one month he was working six twelve-hour days, even taking his meals at the office. He could order whatever food he wanted, the firm picked up the tab, as long as he was at his desk working. The noise at times was deafening, and his cubicle looked as though a windstorm had just passed through. The only image of civility was a five-by-seven photo, thumbtacked to the wall over his desk, taken last summer of the entire family at the beach. He would come home in a foul mood and exhausted. Their marriage suffered.

After the twins were born, it seemed that stress at work accelerated, reaching an intolerable level. Laura was lonely and miserable. He decided he had to get his family back to familiar surroundings and find a job with a more-normal work schedule, even if it meant a cut in pay. Fortunately, his mom and dad loaned them enough to move back to Hartford and to put a down payment on a charming, fiftyish, three-bedroom, one and one-half-bath house scarcely a mile from their home. It was a wide clapboard Cape Cod with bright red shutters that gave it a cozy feel.

Living near the family home provided other comforts as well. Once a week, the kids and Dixie would go to Sam and Julia's for an evening of board games and hot popcorn. Their favorite was Monopoly. Nancy relished looking at family albums and giggled over the flouncy bathing suits that Great Grandma wore to the beach at Coney Island!

For a real treat, sometimes the kids would overnight in sleeping bags in the TV room. Little Aimee would pretend that Dixie was her pony and would try to ride her like a cow-girl. Grandpa Sam insisted that the kids turn off their cell phones for two hours and at bedtime. He had to remind them every time and grew accustomed to their sour faces, but they were soon distracted and quickly became absorbed into the activity of the evening. For Laura and Josh it was their "Get out of jail free card." They could enjoy a leisurely dinner out or a romantic retreat even if it was only for a few hours.

Josh believed that living near his parents would be good for the kids. Laura had been all for it, too. Laura's parents had divorced when she was only three; it left her with a void she seemed only too anxious to fill. She seldom heard from her father. Her mother remarried when she was six, but she never bonded with her stepfather. As the years went by, she somehow became distanced from her mother — something she could never understand or wanted. So becoming part of a new, loving family was a welcome change.

Holidays were always spent at Sam and Julia's, with Josh's two brothers and two sisters. His youngest brother, Edward, was in medical school in Syracuse, and his nearest sibling, Jonathan, graduated UConn with a business major in marketing and was working up the corporate ladder with Connecticut General Life Insurance. Both sisters were older, married with kids, and lived in Connecticut. Every summer saw a family reunion at the shore, hosted by mom and dad.

The big Thanksgiving and Christmas gatherings with all the kids and their families strained their parents' five-bedroom home to its limits. As always, Julia would happily stress herself out in the kitchen each year, trying to outdo the previous holiday. Sam kept the fire going and supervised the kids to ensure they were having fun.

*

Yes, Josh thought, wryly, as he pulled up in front of his modest office and switched off the ignition. *Just one big happy family.*

"Good morning, Jennifer," he said to his secretary as he breezed past her into his dingy office. "Any calls this morning?"

"Not yet, but there are a number of items that need to be addressed from Friday. Here is your agenda for today, and *oh,* you have that new client coming in this afternoon."

Josh nodded and anxiously glanced at the floor. He hesitated, as if to say something. Then he stepped into his private office and closed the door. He hung up his coat with a sigh and riffled through his messages. Most were from his corporate clients, who were becoming more demanding by the month, but he didn't mind, the money was good. He was putting in longer days now at the office and was exploring moving to another office.

He hoped to lease an office in an upscale commercial building where they share a receptionist. It would be a big step for him. Recently he had considered taking on personal injury cases and an occasional divorce, where emotions could run high. But he would be very selective—it had to be a juicy case. Today was to be one of those appointments, a divorce case he simply could not ignore.

This woman had been to three attorneys, who totally

mismanaged her interests. She begged Josh to take her as a client, even tried calling him at home. She was scheduled for an interview this very afternoon at 1:30.

The morning passed quickly and he found himself nervously peering at his watch as the minutes clicked by. As time grew closer to his 1:30 appointment he found himself pacing. Not usually a drinker, Josh kept a dusty bottle of scotch in his desk drawer. He poured a double. At 1:25 he quickly downed it. *One thirty--still no one at the door*, he thought. *Maybe she won't show.*

At precisely 1:33 the door buzzed. Seconds later the secretary announced his 1:30 client.

"Josh, your mother is here."

Two Minus One

Anne Casey

Malady   Malaise   Mortal

                    Malattìa

                          Malo

                    Mal

              Mort

        Muerto

Mòrto

Disease   Decline Dirge   Despair

Fingertips so gifted

Paintbrushes danced at sight of him.

Mind so bright

Easels sprang toward him.

Why him,   WHY him,   Why HIM

          W H Y   H I M

Still filled with sap.

Why not me

Of tiny talent?

Why not me

Now devoid of a childhood.

Motionless, does anyone else hear

my dry heart crack?

A Family's Journey

Charlotte E. Thompson

From *Letters Home*

Writing letters to family and friends is a lovely art we seldom practice in this world of e-mail, voice mail, instant messaging, cell phones, and faxes. Most parents would be in shock if they received an actual letter from one of their kids away at camp or college.

As a busy, practicing pediatrician, I was very fortunate to have a daughter and son who sent letters and cards when they were far away. These helped me through long days of caring for ill and crying children, anxious parents, and turbulent teens. In addition, the letters and cards kept me afloat during a difficult divorce.

Jennifer handmade beautiful cards and wrote only an occasional, special letter. Geoffrey, loving to write, composed wonderful letters that he often illustrated with unusual artwork. The cards and letters were so special that I've saved them all and my frequent rereadings have left them soiled and creased.

Several marked turning points along each of our journeys and a few letters gave me insight into Jennifer and Geoffrey's struggles to find paths right for them, while they searched for the larger meaning of life. Both are now hard-working, creative, and happy adults. E-mails and phone calls have mostly replaced letters, but an occasional special letter is still received and treasured.

The first big step on Jennifer's journey was a brave three-week trip to Honduras, when she was sixteen. The teens, in a non-profit international program, Amigo de las Americas, gave immunizations to children in villages reached on foot or by burro. This was an eye-opening, never-to-be-forgotten experience for Jennifer. Suddenly, she was surrounded by proud, extremely poor people who shared their food and shelters with the teens from another world. This must have seemed far away for Jennifer from her home in the small, affluent town of La Jolla where she grew up.

From Honduras, Jennifer wrote:

Dear Mother,

The first night, after almost 20 hours of traveling, we got to our village in the dead of night. Then after getting situated, we had a confrontation with a soldier with a VERY LARGE GUN on our way to a water hole. You'll be glad to know that now we wait until morning. We eat in an open-air kitchen with the chickens, dogs, and beasties. The kids are beautiful even though they are covered with an inch-thick of dirt. Next week we are going to another village by mule.

Love, Jennifer

The first major step on Geoffrey's journey was as a sixteen-year-old, where he was part of a group traveling to France. First, they had a week's briefing in New York. Then Geoffrey was off to France, where he would spend the summer speaking French with a family in the small town of Ornans.

From Ornans, Geoffrey wrote:

August 8, 1975

Dear Mother,

I am having a great time. I find myself being proud that I am an American and yet loving my association with the French. My French mother took me to visit a very old cathedral today. I found a great deal of pleasure in the cool silence. There was an organ rehearsal while we were there, and the awesomeness of the music seemed to carry more weight than the entire building.

Much love, Geoffrey

In September, Jennifer was off to the University of Colorado to start her freshman year. After she was settled in her dormitory, I received a special, beautiful letter.

Dear Mom,

I want to thank you for writing so often. I know it takes a lot of love and care to be so thoughtful. I enjoy reading all of your letters, and I expectantly wait for their arrival. I really enjoyed the letter I received today with the beautiful rose. I hung it on the wall over my bed. Right now I seem to be extremely tired, and am sitting down, actually writing a letter. I've learned a lot of concepts quickly, both socially and academically; the decision-

*making process of the first freshman month is underway
for me, and I don't seem to be having too many problems
adapting.*

*As I write this letter, I am gradually realizing how
much I miss you as a person, not just as a mother. At this
point, I feel that there are a lot of decisions I will have to
make; I will feel confident in making them knowing that I
will always be supported by your love.*

Much Love, Jennifer

*

With Jennifer in college and Geoffrey deciding to live at his
father's house his senior year in high school, I knew it was time to
start on my own journey. Each of their letters and cards
underscored this and brought me special moments of pleasure.

To find a new path, I needed to locate a job in Northern
California and a pediatrician to take over my much-loved practice.
Jennifer's cards and Geoffrey's letters helped me stay focused on
my goals and some of their courage spilled over into my days. I
finally found both a medical position in northern California and a
pediatrician to take my practice.

When it was time to head north, I backed my tightly packed
car out of the driveway and felt my stomach tied in knots. Fear
was holding me tightly in its grip and I knew I could not turn
back. Placed carefully on the front seat next to me was a poem
Geoffrey had written for the occasion. The poem read:

Sail

till the winds of

your desire fly you to a good harbor.

May each step you take be closer

to your goal.

Though the direction is North of sight,

You always have

A sheltered port in my heart.

I could feel the love and support of his words as I drove north, and glanced frequently at the poem on the seat next to me. It acted as a talisman to guide me safely. I doubt Geoffrey will ever know how important his poem was to me.

Epilogue

Jennifer's and Geoffrey's cards and letters became fewer and fewer as their lives took other directions, and that certainly is how it should be. Their cards and letters are like a handful of golden nuggets I can reach for and hold tightly during times of loneliness or when the world seems to be spinning out of balance.

These *Letters Home* have seen me through many dark days on my journey and helped me realize the most important thing any of us can do, as we make our way in the world, is to develop and keep close, enduring connections with family members and friends. Letters and cards help maintain these connections, and to lose the art of writing *Letters Home* would be a loss indeed.

As I think about the richness of Jennifer and Geoffrey's cards and letters, I realize how fortunate I have been. In many ways, my life has been difficult, with much work and little extra money. Yet having Jennifer and Geoffrey's support has made an enormous difference. By choice, I have followed an independent path with the only constraints being financial ones. This has allowed me to live my life as honestly and fully as I wished.

No, I have not found answers to many of my questions, but have decided that peace and fulfillment are the first important steps on my journey and that perhaps there are no final answers. I know that I could not have fulfilled half of my dreams without Jennifer and Geoffrey's support, so vividly portrayed by their cards and letters. These truly are a treasure chest of shining jewels that can be opened when I feel the need. My hope is that by sharing these special *Letters Home* love and warmth will be brought to readers.

Robert Epstein says that:

"Letters are acts of faith, because in a letter I disclose myself, I open my heart, trusting that the other will read and respond likewise with an open heart. Letters are seeds planted in an open heart that may one day grow into tall trees and, like trees, a sturdy letter can last a lifetime."

I agree wholeheartedly with these words and hope my readers will want to take their pens in hand and try deepening and enriching their own lives by writing *Letters Home.*

*

How grateful I am to have Jennifer's beautiful cards and letters. She died from breast cancer on April 18, 2011. It was a painful, terrible loss.

Grow to Love

Bradley Collins

Olivia wiggled impatiently in the airport chair. Her parents were returning from Guadalajara. As her grandma held her little brother Daniel, she stared at the sliding door where passengers come out. "Calmate mi'ja," Grandma said. "They'll be here soon."

"I can't calm down, Abuela. I'm too excited!"

"Esta bien, mi'ja," Grandma replied. "Hold Daniel's hand. Vamonos."

Olivia watched every passenger come out. Each was greeted by friends or family with joyful hugs. Finally, Olivia squealed with delight. She had spotted her mother Isabella's long black hair flowing over her left shoulder as only she wore it. She ran and jumped into her arms. "Oh, Mommy I missed you so much!" She hugged her mother tightly, who whispered something in her daughter's ear. Olivia looked up obediently at her stepfather's pink, sunburned face and mumbled, "And you too… Daddy."

"We missed you too, sweetie." Her stepfather, Walter, kissed the top of her head.

"What'd ya bring us?" asked Daniel.

"¡Ay, niño, your manners!" Grandma chastised.

"Sorry, Abue'. Welcome home you guys."

"Thanks Dannies. We did find you something, but it can wait until we get home," Isabella answered exhaustedly.

Once they settled at home, Isabella gave her son a small brown box. "Daniel, this is *un balero*. It's a game that has been played by kids your age for over four hundred years. It is handmade from Zapopan. I hope you like it."

"Awesome, thanks Mom!" Daniel bounced to his room, swinging the colorful wooden ball on a string and trying to catch it on its handle. Isabella looked at her husband, who pulled out a larger box from their luggage.

"Olivia, I found this for you." Her dark- brown eyes widened with anticipation as she reached out both arms for the package. "Careful, sweetie. It's heavy." She wondered what amazing gifts could come in such a heavy box. With some fatherly assistance, she got the top open and stared inside. Her excited smile morphed into an expression of blank confusion. "Well, pull it out! Here, let me help you." Walter lifted from the top, revealing a gorgeous ceramic pot, bright with colorful paintings of flowers and designs.

"¡Que bonita!" Grandma gasped.

"He really did find the most beautiful one there," her mother encouraged. Olivia did her best to follow her mother's cue and hid her disappointment.

"Wow, it's so pretty, Thank you so much!" She forced a smile. "And it has… dirt?"

"Well, yes, but it is more than that," Walter explained. "This is a hand-painted *talavera* from Tonalá, and inside is a root of a Mexican flame vine. This will grow to be more beautiful every year, just like you. We packed it in some soil from your great grandfather's garden, and I even blessed it with a drop of holy water from Catedral de Guadalajara. If you learn to trim it, and care for it, it can grow anywhere you want it to!"

"Oh." Olivia paused. "Thanks. I love my pot. Of dirt." She reached up and kissed Walter's cheek awkwardly, and carried the pot to the patio. She set it in the corner, and ran to her room. Walter looked at Isabella and shrugged sadly.

"It's okay, Amor. Your heart was in the right place."

"Yeah. Maybe she'll grow to love it."

That night, Olivia lay in bed wondering about the gift from her stepfather. She thought, *Why not a pretty dress, or some candy? ¿No muñeca? ¿No marioneta? Just a stupid pot of dirt? He doesn't love me at all. And I have to trim it? He gave me a chore! ¡Que malo, I hate it!* Too upset to sleep, she buried her tears in her pillow.

Over the next few months, Olivia ignored the pot. Despite her lack of attention, the talavera caught a few rays of sun in its corner each day, and stray drops of water from a leaky hose nearby. It sprouted, and began to grow straight up the side of the patio fence.

As the vine grew and wrapped around the top of the fence, Olivia would look away and pretend not to see it. But then one day, as she walked home from school, the blooms had multiplied so much she couldn't keep from staring in awe. The first blooms had become deep reddish flowers. They were surrounded by younger blooms, which were an explosive shade of light orange, over shiny leaves of dark hunter-green. Two butterflies and a hummingbird danced among the flowers. The patio looked magical, like it was lit up for a fiesta.

Whoa. Pretty cool. This was Olivia's first positive thought about her gift. Later that week she saw her stepfather trimming the vines. She felt guilty, and decided to show some interest. "Whatchya doin' Daddy?

"Well, this vine kinda' picked the top of the fence, but now its trying to spread everywhere. We'll trim it and hopefully tame it. I could use some help, if you want?" Olivia stayed and learned how to trim by her stepfather's side.

After a few more months she noticed it had crawled up the side of the house toward her bedroom window. "Daddy, why didn't you keep the vine from climbing up to the roof?" she asked.

"Well, sweetie, it was blessed for you, remember? I just thought, why not see where it goes? Besides, I happen to think the sun shines brightest on my baby girl. Maybe your flowers agree."

Olivia felt warmth in her heart, and smiled a smile that could not be hidden. From then on, she cared for the vine daily. She transplanted sections of it around the rock wall that outlined their yard, the trellis over their front walk, and the steep slope at the west edge of their property that went almost straight down to the sidewalk below. It surrounded her bedroom window on its own, and lit up all areas where she tended to it. The vine flourished, and gave her place in this world a special, fiery glow.

Honeybees loved the flowers' pollen, so Olivia and her stepfather took on a beekeeping project together. This turned into a small group of hives, and they shared the sweetest honey with their neighbors. When some people showed an interest, they taught them how to keep their own hives.

Isabella started composting with the vine trimmings, and shared her method with other neighborhood moms who noticed her successful garden. She also started a butterfly project with Daniel. They found caterpillars and butterfly chrysalides on the vines, and made terrariums with vine sprigs to give to neighboring children as gifts. Daniel even found his own project. He searched online and found a simple way to make hummingbird feeders, which also spread through the neighborhood like wildfire.

With all these projects stemming from the Mexican flame vine, Olivia's community became a unique one. She shared her plant, which lit up many homes. Honeybees, butterflies, and hummingbirds pollinated the most beautiful and fruitful gardens in the county, and the composting made them the most fertile. The animal projects fostered learning and brought kids together. Families were eager to share their harvest with each other, and many new friendships grew.

Years later, Olivia came home from the university because her stepfather was ill. She rushed past the talavera full of blooms on the table to hug her dad. "Daddy I've missed you. Are you okay?"

"I'll be fine," Walter said with a cough. "Just some virus, and a little fever's all."

The beautiful young woman thought for a moment. "I researched our vines for a biology paper. They're called *senecio confuses*, from the *asteraceae* family. There are other types in South America, and they make remedies with them." She worked vigorously, boiling a teapot to infuse some vine roots, fresh flower petals, and flame vine honey.

Walter smiled, listening to his daughter talk about her life. When it was ready, he sipped her concoction and felt better almost instantly. Olivia sat down, relieved. She put her head on her father's shoulder, gazed at the table, and began to weep. "Daddy, I didn't even like that pot when you gave it to me. I was mad because it wasn't a doll or a dress. How did you know it would help me so much? I learned to work hard, to be giving, to love nature, to help others, all those things."

"Well, sweetie, I didn't really know any of that. I just said a little prayer and let God do the rest."

"You did? What prayer?"

"The wish of every parent, I guess. I prayed that I could help you have a good life, and that you could discover it and make it your own. And you're doing just that. I'm so proud, I love you so much, mi'ja."

Walter kissed his daughter on the top of the head. Olivia felt warmth in her heart that glowed as brightly as her own special place in this world.

The Void The Void

Wayne Williams

Death is looking me in the face
he hurts, he pains, he weakens
I know Death is male, because how would a woman
Take me away like this?"

So why did I enjoy life so much
Just to have this happen?
All those travels, adventures, and beauties of the heart
Extreme delicacies at tongues' edges,
Those kind smiles and great favors,
A massage, then another massage,

The whispers of smooth lines in tomes
Of poetry written by the box-full
The awards, honors, recognition
Were once here and are now so far away

I lay in my bed sweating, cognizant of mortality
More than ever before
Wishing for little more
Than to go to my garden and pick tomatoes

My dearest wife loves me; I am such a lucky guy.

Perhaps I won't die today

But this is as good a moment as any.

I'd rather wait awhile, however to join up with the ancestors

Come on — give me another fifty years!

Where's the whiskey?

A fine medicine indeed

Here's a salute to all of you.

The Happening

Gary Winters

Alan Kaprow first used the word in 1959. He said, "A Happening is an assemblage of events, performed or perceived in more than one time and place. Its material environments may be constructed, taken over directly from what is available, or altered slightly; just as its activities may be invented or commonplace...It is art but seems closer to life."

The posters read, PLASTIC GRASS: A HAPPENING, Seaview, Fire Island, New York. A large crowd showed up at the picturesque white-sand beach next to the city junkyard. I had thrown stuff from the junkyard over the fence onto the beach; a stove, lamps, bottles, an ironing board. I put garden tools on the sand; a flat of eggs, shaving cream, red spray paint, plywood, an old broom. Over the entrance I strung a nine-by twelve-foot American flag.

The spectators standing in the warm sun finally figured out they weren't going to be entertained. Children dug in the sand with the shovel and then got the bright idea for an egg toss. See if you could catch the egg without getting it all over your face. A man advanced on the Tappen gas range with a sledgehammer, screaming about how he'd had it with his wife's cooking.

The *Fire Island News* reported the scene: "A girl in a blue diaphanous dress was encouraging him. 'That one's for the rich,' the girl shouted as the young man raised the hammer and brought it down with a violent clang on the white metal. 'And that one's for the fuzz,' she screamed as one of the front burners caved in. Then she anointed him with shaving cream."

Someone set a huge blaze in one of the toilets. "A kid could catch on fire," a parent exclaimed. A television antenna poked out of a mound of sand where a dark-haired girl was buried. Two blond girls were reading to her out of the Manhattan telephone book. A man sweeping the sand put the broom down, picked up the sledgehammer and ran to the stove, yelling, "I hate fried rice."

A small, redheaded boy with shaving cream on his face observed the man's attack on the appliance. Afterward the boy said they both felt much better.

A bleached blonde in a flowery print dress and gold sandals said to her husband, "*Your* son just set fire to the American flag." A firecracker exploded in the toilet. A female voice cried out, "Someone is gonna get *killed*." More firecrackers went off. A young girl in a bikini spray-painted on the plywood, "God is alive. He is in Argentina."

All day people came and left, but then came back again.

The sunset glittered on the sea like sprinkled stardust in the little tinsel playground for world-class movers and shakers. Everyone felt like they had been part of a real Happening and that, somehow, things were never going to be the same.

A Little Cold Duck in a Cold War

Sam Warren

"Hey Jack," Col. Jim Spair, the U.S. Army attaché, asked his companion, Col. Jack Waterman, the Air Attaché with the Canadian Embassy in Moscow, USSR, in 1967, in the middle of the cold war. "Are we getting any closer to that new Russian winery they wanted us to visit?"

The two colonels were on a road trip through the Russian countryside.

"I think it's just past that next village ahead. I wish we could have driven one of the Embassy's Plymouth station wagons instead of this damn Volga. You would think that a country that could put a satellite into space could build a decent car."

The clunky Volga was one of two cars manufactured in Russia in those days. The other was the luxurious Zil that was only for top party members. The Zil, which was a Packard in everything but name. As the Russians bought the entire Packard factory, including all their dies and shipped it to the USSR, the only thing different was the emblem on the hood.

In those days, the Russians let us take trips into their countryside in exchange for us allowing them to do the same in the U.S. Of course they made sure that we never got close to anything of real interest. However, we got to see how the agriculture was getting along and they couldn't hide everything. Little bits of intelligence all added up if you knew what to look for. One example was that we all took overexposed pictures so as to see the underbellies of vehicles in order to read their serial numbers. With a number of photos, the CIA people in Foggy Bottom back in Washington, D.C., could figure out Soviet production of certain items.

"I still think it's a waste of time, I don't think we can learn anything from their wine-making, but anything to make them happy," Jim said, pulling up at the end of the long gravel driveway where they were welcomed by a small group of officials from the winery.

"Welcome to our humble People's winery, Tavarish," the official said in Russian. "Come inside and see if our wine is equal to your California wine."

There is a rule for members of the Embassy traveling outside of Moscow. To prevent both parties from being poisoned, you never ate together at the same place and at the same time. However, in this case it would have been impolite for one to refuse.

In spite of Jim and Jack's feeling that something else was going on that they didn't know about, they had a pleasant time eating some of the local bread and cheese and drinking the local wine— that is, until they started to feel sick.

"Jim, I think we had better head back to the car. I think they put something in that wine. My stomach feels really queasy."

They excused themselves and headed back to their car, but before they got there, Jim heaved up his stomach over his shoes and Jack followed suit. It was a bit messy, but Jack had the presence of mind to keep the shoe as it was evidence of what happened. Hoping not to pass out, they made it to their car and headed back to their hotel in the nearby town. They barely made it to their room before passing out on their beds fully dressed.

*

Late the next morning, Jim slowly opened his eyes. "Oh my head," he moaned. "What was in that wine?" Looking around, he suddenly sat up. *What the hell am I doing nude next to Jack in the same bed?*

All around the room there were empty wine bottles and cigarette butts, but the vomit was all cleaned up. *What the hell was the KGB thinking? It must have been a local officer who thought this one up. Even with the pictures I'm sure they took, no one is going to believe that two distinguished-looking senior attaches from the American and Canadian Embassies would have a homosexual orgy in the middle of a fact-finding mission.*

He shook his friend to wake him up. Jack sat up with a start, staring at the surroundings and having a hard time believing what he saw. He laughed when he saw Jim next to him in the nude. "Boy, we must have had a good time last night."

"Let's pack," Jack said. "We had better cut our trip short and head back to Moscow to have the Embassy doctor pump out our stomachs. It's a good thing they forgot to clean out the vomit from my shoe, so we should be able to get some proof that we were poisoned. But first get your camera out and let's take some of our own pictures."

*

The Russians never did publish the photos, but the American and Canadian Embassies did.

They made the *International Herald Tribune*, where it was a top story and an embarrassment to the KGB. I wonder what happened to the local KGB official who thought up this plot. Siberia comes to mind.

As you might have guessed, this is a true story that happened in 1967 in the middle of the Cold War.

Drippy Pants

Alan Converse

Mom chatted on the phone with Mrs. Kuhn.

"Ayuh," she said with a smile at me. "They do, do they? Well, I guess Hal can go...mmm let me see..." She glanced coyly at me.

I danced around waiting for the answer. Mom usually wouldn't let me go up the street to get a Fudgesicle, but Kuhnnie and I had it figured out. If his Mom asked my Mom if I could go with him, she always agreed.

"OK, I'll give him a nickel and send him over in a minute." She turned to me with a fake frown on her face. "Go change your pants and I'll give you the nickel."

I crossed the dusty road, kicking sand with my bare feet. I had a nickel in the pocket of my drippy pants. Johnny Kuhn was waiting for me in front of his house holding his nickel and pointing at his drippy pants.

We headed up the dirt ruts feeling the warm dust squeeze between our toes, up toward where the asphalt started. The candy store was a block further up the street.

We laughed with anticipation, forgetting about our aborted project to pave our end of the street. A half-hour before we had been smoothing the side of Harkness Avenue with the same old worn-out spoons that we had used to dig to China, until that project petered out. We were smoothing the dust, somehow thinking that if we could smooth that part of the road someone would come and pave it. As the infrequent cars drove by, we waved and yelled at them.

"Keep to the right, keep to the right."

We didn't want them to mess up the part we had already smoothed. After one car had passed a bit too close, rutting part of our newly smoothed roadbed, Johnnie threw down his spoon, saying, "Let's get Fudgesicles! I'll ask my mom!"

Now, the bald man behind the counter saw us coming and dug out the Fudgesicles from the open-top freezer. "That's right kids. One nickel right here on the barrelhead buys you a Fudgesicle."

We grabbed them eagerly, wondering if the wooden handles had the word FREE printed on them. We had heard such a stick was worth a free Fudgesicle.

As we walked back, the dripping fudge fell all over our pants. Life can't be better than walking home on a New England summer day with a Fudgesicle, even if you can't eat it fast enough and most of it melts away.

*

I thought of those old sticky drippy pants and wondered what had happened to them. Mom was long gone, lost to Alzheimer's several years ago. I gazed at the old Cape Cod cottage the family had moved into when it was brand new after the World War. It looked the same, but at some point in the past, the owners had added a breezeway and a garage. It had a crisp new coat of paint and dormers in the roof. Someone had probably finished the attic into bedrooms like many of the post-war Cape Cods in the area.

My mind drifted back. There were other things to do in those days: dirt clod fights, playing cowboys and Indians with cap pistols, or baseball on the vacant lot. Whatever happened? Other generations now text their friends and play computer games instead of throwing dirt clods and shooting cap pistols. Little League replaced sandlot ball. Kids buy Slurpees instead of Fudgesicles. Harkness Avenue is all paved and the traffic rushes by.

Sudden Death

Mardie Schroeder

She had come a long way and encountered obstacles she never knew existed and wasn't prepared for. It was hard going. Her stamina was fading fast. She couldn't make headway on the slick, slippery slopes she faced. Walking on the flat part was not a problem. It was slick but she could manage it without falling. But every attempt to climb the steep glistening incline was thwarted. She would only get so far and then her legs gave out and she collapsed back to where she started.

Her long slender legs were tired and she had to rest before another attempt. Would she ever get out of this predicament?

She slowly and tentatively walked to another part of the insurmountable mountain. She didn't know what was on the other side but she knew there was nothing for her where she was stranded.

Another futile attempt had her tumbling back down onto the slick surface.

It became light. Perhaps she could now see where she could gain a foothold. But looking around she could see no vantage point.

She thought of all she had left behind for this foolish trek.

What had she hoped to gain? Was there any reason for her actions?

She heard a noise but couldn't place where it came from. Then another louder boom and she felt a drop of water find its mark near her. Then more drops made a patter of staccato notes on the slick surface.

That was the last thing she heard as an avalanche of water crushed her, carrying her across the shiny flat expanse into a whirling eddy and down a long dark tunnel into an abyss, dissolving her miniscule body into nothingness.

Race Games

Ty Piz

There are places away from the crowds where bright colored flags and the spectacle of race teams do not exist. No magazine journalists, no trophies for the showcase or paychecks to win. It's in this silence where riders go to develop their skills, test themselves and just play-ride with buddies.

Outside of Denver, at the foot of Lookout Mountain, there's a rock quarry that has become our playground. The floor is pulverized rock, turned into powdery sand from years of tractors, bulldozers and dump-truck traffic. Today, our group includes Big Red, McGoo, Ziggy, Too Tall, G-Glaze, brother Ron, and Tiger — that's me.

Big Red wheelies around the final bend of our homemade motocross track looking for more challenge. As he revs his mighty 360 Bultaco, we sit at the bottom of a sixty-foot mountain of rock with a 70-degree face and watch in awe. Three-quarters up the steep grade there's a ledge, and we can no longer see the top of the mountain.

Brrrraaaap, Big Red feathers the clutch out, his rear tire digs in and he launches five feet above the plateau and lands safely.

Ziggy fires up his 250 Honda. He snaps the throttle open and selects the ideal line for his attack up the jagged hill. He lets the clutch fly and digs his way up. Reaching the ledge, his Honda nearly vertical, he takes off into the serenity of blue sky and disappears.

Where is he? A moment of panic. *Did the bike go upside down on the ledge?*

He reappears, his weight on the back of the seat as his Honda shoots over the top and lands.

Whew, he made it!

The thunder of McGoo's Honda reverberates through the canyon as he zips up the rock face and disappears. My pulse stops cold with the unearthly silence. McGoo clears the ledge. While in midair he tilts the bike into a cross-up posture, lands, and slides to a magnificent stop, covering us in dust. Grinning ear to ear, he removes his goggles, his eyes aglow.

We're atop the plateau now. Too Tall fires up his CZ-400. "Let's rumble, boys." On a mission to outdo the others, Too Tall turns his beast, a quick ride an additional twenty feet further up the trail. He checks out the landscape: sagebrush, dirt, rocks, and the disheartening drop over the face that is now seventy feet high.

Suddenly, he's moving. First gear, second, rooster-tailing dirt, he's frigging flying. *It's too fast, man, back down!*

He races toward the edge of dark clay and launches into the emptiness of blue sky. He clears the ledge and disappears from view! A clean leap for him.

G-Glaze prances to the edge with confidence and takes his

look. Brrrraaaap, dust peels off the rear tire from his 501 Maico. Effortless motion, no other way to describe the way he rides. A spotless jump.

My turn. It's lonely up here. A shiver streams down my spine. Heavy breath in, and a heavier sigh out. My feet shake upon the gnarled pegs, I wiggle my fingers over the soft rubber grips. Tighten abs, rolling my shoulders I tiptoe along the edge. *Oh shit this is high. They've all made it.* I ride another five feet up the trail. *Looks doable.* I nod to the boys below. My takeoff on the peppy Yamaha 125 is fast. The exhilaration to midflight is quick. Earth, sky, wind, earth, the landing is spine-jarring. *Crap, didn't think I was going to clear the ledge.*

Looking upward four stories to the edge, McGoo appears entranced by the gigantic mountain. We watch as he rolls by. His drive is swift, sailing up and over the ledge, he nails the landing, hollering with a big grin. That's our McGoo.

We look to one another. Who's next to climb this bloodthirsty demon?

I don't want to be last so I kick-start my Bumblebee and bring her to life. Ring, ding-ding, ring ding-ding. First gear, second, click into third. As I race with maximum velocity, the suspension collapses as I make contact with the mountainside. Her buzz stirs my fingers, making my heart pound. I speed up the face. *Okay, this is good.* The protrusion approaches. Big launch. *Aw-shit.* In midair my breath freezes, and my muscles flex. *Come on arms, press the bars forward. Press harder!*

The front tire hits. *CRACK!* The engine rpm's spin and instinctively my body leans forward. Rear tire goes ka-thud, spinning with no traction to drive onward.

Oh shit, I didn't push enough to reach the plateau. I'm tumbling backwards. Sky in front of me, sky behind. *I'm screwed.*

My Bumblebee grabs a bite of dusty terrain. I tip sideways and she leans into the hillside. I dab my foot down, it slams into the rocky soil. Electrical impulses shoot through my leg. Throttle wide open, another bite into the dark clay. She lurches forward. *Come on, girl, just two more inches to bring us out of this crap.*

Grabbing the grips with all my might, I squeeze the seat with my knees to hang on tighter, chest perched against the fuel tank. *We've cleared it, girl!* Trembles run like a wildfire throughout my body. *We're alive, Bumblebee!*

I see Ron and other boys riding up the access trail. *Suppose we've pushed the envelope far enough today.* High fives and handshakes, then we ride back to the pits to load the bikes. It's been an awesome day.

*

It's early spring. The days of spinning doughnuts in the snow have passed. We're in our late-forties now, and I find a break in my busy schedule to go visit my buddy McGoo. He's been in a wheelchair for over twenty years and now he's at Craig Rehabilitation Hospital.

"Hey McGoo. Let's go for a stroll to the park."

"It's not happenin', Tiger!"

"Maybe lift weights at Club USA like we used to?"

"Nah, I'll just watch the Light-Rail zoom by."

"It's really weird."

"What's that, Tiger?"

"Why do people think that by stuffing their zippy cars in front of me so I can't merge that they'll get to their destinations so much quicker? Do those two seconds really alter their course of travel?"

"Give it up, man! Those people will never know the buzz we get every time we put a wheel on the track."

"Come-on, McGoo, doesn't everyone live in micro-seconds? If I go two seconds deeper into my brake markers, how much distance can I gain over the racer in front of me?"

"That depends," he says. "At 80 mph about 115 feet. Racing at 140, close to 220 feet."

"So when I'm at Daytona doing a buck-eighty, I'll pass through an entire football field in just one tick of the clock. That's a buzz!"

"Yeah, you go two seconds beyond your normal brake marker you'll be out in the weeds." He laughs.

"A lot can happen in two seconds."

I move my chair closer to his hospital bed.

"Let's look at two beats of your heart. Your average is 86

BPM. That's about two beats every three seconds. I wonder how much oxygen the red blood cells receive in those three seconds?"

"Stop it. That's too scientific for me, man."

"Okay, McGoo. Just breathe. Eat some mashed potatoes, enjoy that apple pie the nurse brought you."

"Tiger, what's it all mean?"

"What if I say... 'I do!'"

"What are you talking about?"

"When Robyn and I got married, I said, 'I do!' That's about two seconds."

"I suppose so. What's your point?"

"Those two seconds changed our world forever."

"Sure did. For the better, my friend!"

"Hey, McGoo. I know you miss the buzz of racing."

"Hell yeah! Tiger, you seem lost. What's up?"

"Racing's been the force that drives me to find out how fast I can really be. It's hard to step away."

"You can let it go. You've done great these last couple years."

"Not me. McGoo, you were a freakin' awesome racer. Sorry that nasty crash made the decision for you."

"Yeah, now that damn wheelchair is the only wheels I'll ride."

We both stare at the grey chair in the corner.

"We should go celebrate our Sagittarius birthdays again this year."

"No partying for me. I signed the papers today."

"What papers?"

"Organ donor papers."

"That's good. My brother Dirk was a donor. And Robyn got 40 more wonderful years because her family donated their kidneys to her. You'll help somebody live better, like you did with my racing."

"It was a hoot, Tiger."

"You helped me learn the fast lines."

"Nah, you did all that. I was just there to watch."

"Remember those days at the dirt hills."

"Yeah, we did jump some gnarly stuff at the clay pits."

We embrace, and tears flow.

"Go get em', Tiger."

"Peace always, McGoo."

*

Through the years we've made many excursions to the clay pits with family and friends who came to play-ride and share the freedom of flying over the peak of the mountains.

Brrrraaaap!

Making Peace: Step by Step

Anne Hoiberg

As many of us toasted the New Year in January, we also rejoiced about the possibility of peace. With the end of the Iraq War and the near conclusion of the twelve-year war in Afghanistan, we were given the hope that we, as a nation, were finally finished with war; and soon it would become passé. We wanted to believe that by now, our nation had learned painful lessons from the tragic brutality of the 20th Century and that of the early 21st Century. Many of us agree that war is never the answer.

There are those of us who also believe that the leadership that commands the U.S. Army and Marines heard the national cry: "No Boots on the Ground." This assumption first surfaced at the time of the Libyan airstrikes in 2011. It continues with each proposed military action, such as in Syria and Iran.

With the recent renewal of an increased presence in Iraq, we, the people, have been assured by our national leaders in their frequent media pronouncements, that there will be "No Boots on the Ground." Can we really put our faith in this recurring statement? Dare we believe that, as a national mandate, it is gaining traction day by day with the decision-makers? Those same media accounts reverberate with the pain and suffering of our wounded and emotionally damaged men and women of the armed forces who appear exhausted—tired of the wars and the consequences. We, the people, also seem to be suffering from battle fatigue.

An intriguing solution to ending war centers on whether it is possible to capitalize on the repetition of a phrase as a means to achieve that goal. If our strategy is to stop sending our troops into harm's way, then, it would follow that our first step requires total commitment to the mandate: "No Boots on the Ground."

In repeating this directive as the immediate response to any declaration about invading a country, the words might produce the reality. We must counter all suggestions of war with, "No Boots on the Ground."

There can be no "next big war" as has been predicted to occur in the Middle East. We, the people, must be adamant about "No Boots on the Ground."

Once this rallying cry becomes entrenched and is a solid platform under our feet, our next step may be to deliver another mandate: "No Military Killing Drones in the Sky."

Step by repetitious step, we, the people, if united in our vision and action, will advance toward the goal we all want—peace—in our time.

A Little Night Music

Barbara Crothers

Fred answers the phone and turns to me, "It's Sheridan." He listens for a bit, then says, "He and Betsey have invited the family down for a post-Yule gathering and wants to know if we would like to go." Fred puts his hand over the mouthpiece and looks over the top of his glasses, "Do you want to go to Manzanillo for New Year's? Norm, Dick, and Mom will be there too."

"Uh, well, if you think we can get ready in time . . . what else does he want?"

Freddy shrugs his shoulders, "Uh, just a TV, a phone, some Wheat Chex, corn and, ah, oh yeah, some applesauce."

So here we are, driving into the desert under millions of stars with no man-made lights to mask their beauty.

The desert stretches for miles; hot and dusty, bone-dry, cactus-filled miles, with few stops and a road under construction from San Diego to Hermosillo, Sonora, Mexico.

In the distance, I see a motel sign. The place looks fresh, well-tended and the aroma of jasmine fills the hot night air. "How about we stop here, I'm hot, tired and need a shower. You must be tired too, Darlin'. It's almost ten o'clock," I say to my husband. He gives an affirmative nod.

"If there's a vacancy let's stay, but you know how it is around

New Year's Eve." Fred drives toward the motel. It has a nice, plastered, cement-block fence and a wrought-iron gate you can see through. Each room has a garage with a dark curtain gathered on one side, probably to protect the car in heavy rain or wind. Just beyond the gate, near the bougainvillea hedge, a young man stands and motions for us to move forward. Fred turns into the yard, slows the pickup and rolls down the window.

The attendant says, "*Nueve mil pesos, por favor.*" Fred hands him a $10,000 peso note. The attendant smiles and says, "*Lo siento, no tengo cambio* (Sorry, I don't have change)."

"Okay, no problem," Fred says over his shoulder and follows behind another guy who directs us into a garage. The *joven* (young man) pulls the curtain across the garage opening behind us, turns and runs back toward the front gate. Fred parks the pickup; we get out, take our bags and walk up two steps leading into the room.

"Oh, Darlin', we didn't get a receipt . . . don't you think we should ask for one?" I say while going into the room. The jasmine, the cooler night air and a huge, almost-full moon sheds its pale light over the red bank of bougainvilleas; I begin to relax.

"No, not now, I'm tired, need a shower, get into my 'jams and lie down for a while; I'll get a receipt when we check out in the morning."

The room is clean and has a nice smell; sort of citrusy. The bed is on a foot-high platform and both the bed and platform are covered with a heavy red and black bedspread, like an altar or a king's lounge or one of those velvet paintings above the back bar in a saloon.

I look around, put my bag on a folding rack near the door to the bathroom. "Well, this is really interesting. It could be a place for a tryst; a lovers' rendezvous — would you look at this? There's a bidet in there!" I say from the bathroom.

"You're kidding me; all of this for about ten bucks and a small tip? Wow! You're right, though." He gives me *that* look, raises his eyebrows and smiles, ". . . and we thought the honeymoon was over!"

Laughing, we put our things away; Fred showers and comes into the room with a towel around his waist, "The shower shoots out a stream of water like a firehose, but it's good and hot."

"Then I guess it's better than that place we stayed once on the other side of town where the guy told us to 'just press your body against the wall' where the shower was supposed to be; you remember, where the water just dribbled down the wall and he said the owner wouldn't give our money back and we'd have to stay there?" I wink and say through a mouthful of toothpaste while brushing my teeth, "I really should have splurged on a sexy negligee for this divine place," and rinse the dust out of my mouth with the bottled mineral water we brought with us. "I won't be long," I say as I close the bathroom door.

It is late, but everything seems perfect so far. Going through

Mexicali shaved almost a hundred miles off the trip; the road not bad and no animals on the highway. The Isuzu tallied a respectable 37 miles per gallon, and the sky: drop-dead gorgeous.

The shower revitalizes me and I towel-dry my hair. Fred opens the bottle of pinot noir from the case we keep in back of the pickup. He pours the wine into our stemmed glasses. He raises his glass, peers through it and says in his most authentic Bogart voice, "Here's lookin' at you, kid."

He turns on the TV first, but then finds some soft, ages-old, romantic music on the radio. "Moon Glow"floods the room in our found nest along Highway15 south of the border.

After the wine is gone, I close my eyes and, like turning down a rheostat, I sleep. Fred takes longer to relax, and naps fitfully. Generally he rests for three to five hours a night, depending on the situation and his state of awareness. He is alert at the slightest sound, whereas I wake if something is different, out of context. We are in a motel, where people come and go at odd hours, so I rest easily. He tries to spare me his wakefulness. I am grateful for his concern.

Sounds scream through the walls! We awaken brutally. It is 2:45 a.m. Music is blasting in the room next door. Fred is standing on the bed between our pillows with a tennis shoe in hand, pounding on the wall adjoining the next room.

"That. Music. Has. Been. Blasting. For. Over. An. Hour." His words expelled in cadence to the sole of his shoe hitting the wall.

Then silence.

He lies down and begins to rest, "I hear water running next door . . . now heavy footsteps . . ." He turns toward me, ". . . light, high-heeled footsteps."

"There, Darlin', it sounds like they're leaving. I think that quiet click was the door closing," I whisper as I stuff a pillow under my head and pull the sheet up. The roar of an engine echoes in the adjoining garage.

"Goshdangit! Now there's the door again." Fred says through bared teeth.

I hear a couple of female voices in the room next door, but can't make out the words.

"Does it sound to you like a couple of women are in there straightening up the room . . . in the middle of the night?" Whispering now, I move closer to him. "Would anyone do that? Listen! Yes, they're making the bed; they're giggling!" We both turn over and try to sleep.

"Good Lord!" Fred covers his head with the pillow. "Now they vacuum the floor and turn on the water to wash something and listen to the radio and talk to each other?"

I listen to them; they sing a bit and laugh a little. The room must be almost set aright; there is no sound now except for the click of the door closing.

We awake, grumbling; it is 6:30 a.m. The bags are packed; we heave ourselves into the day. He grabs me around the waist, takes my bag from me and nuzzles my neck; I have to smile a little and then a lot.

"Are you mad at me?" Fred pushes me playfully. "Are you mad at me? I know how you hate to miss your beauty rest." I have to smile; we laugh out loud.

"We'll just forget the receipt, okay?" I say as we move out onto the highway. I look over at him, the grumpiness gone now, and say, "I didn't know that about you, Freddy . . ."

"What's that?" he says from the driver's seat.

"Oh, you know, the standing on the bed, tennis shoe pounding . . ."

*

A few years later, while telling of that night in Hermosillo, we learned there are motels referred to as "retiros." These motels rent by the hour; the vehicles are hidden behind dark, pulled-across-the-opening-curtains and have nothing to do with wind or rain. No identities are disclosed. All transactions are in cash, there are no receipts or ledgers for signatures; the rooms are cleaned after the tenants leave. We learned the ten dollars we paid for the room should have paid for the first hour!

The Pajamas

Caroline McCullagh

June 2007

Pablo and I exited the elevator on the sixth floor of Briggs Hall on the campus of the University of California, San Diego. He ran ahead, reading the numbers on the office doors.

"Pablo, slow down." I smiled in apology to the two male students who walked toward me.

"Here it is, *Abuelita,* six-one-eight," he said, pointing. I followed him through the door.

Jack stood by the desk hugging a woman . . . No . . . Kissing her!

"*Abuelito,* we're here," Pablo said.

The woman turned, her hand on Jack's arm. "Well, who's this?" she asked in that smarmy voice some adults use with children.

Jack didn't blush—although it's hard to tell because of his tan skin. "This is my grandson, Pablo."

"Pablo," she said. "Aren't you the handsome young man with your nice curly black hair. How old are you?"

"I'm six. I had my birthday."

"Well, what a big boy you are. And is this your nanny?" She looked at me for the first time.

Nanny indeed!

"No, this is my abuelita."

"Abuelita? I don't know that word. Does it mean the same as nanny?"

"Not nanny," Jack said. "It's Spanish for grandmother. This is my wife, Anne. Anne, my friend Deirdre Bernard."

Friend.

"Ah, Jack, I didn't know you'd remarried. How nice to meet you, Anne." She took her hand off him and held it out to me.

I wanted to rip it off her arm.

Deirdre looked fortyish, a well-maintained fortyish—an easy twenty years younger than I. She had long, silky blonde hair—no dark roots—halfway down her back. When she'd turned to see who we were, it swirled like in one of those damned shampoo commercials. Slender and five-foot-eight in her spike heels, she stood as tall as Jack. Without those heels, she'd be pretty close to my five-five. Her draped, low-cut, emerald-green silk blouse barely concealed her substantial breasts. And the absolute worst thing? Her long, manicured fingernails—bright red.

Jack loves nail polish.

"Are you taking an anthropology class?" I asked.

She laughed and shook her head. "Oh, no. I teach anthropology too. My office is next door. What a nice surprise that Jack's here now."

"Yes, isn't it. How do you know Jack?"

"I taught at Carleton University a long time ago—my first job after I earned my Ph.D."

I had a flash of insight. I knew who she was. *Shit!*

"How interesting," I said, without one bit of sincerity. "We'll have to talk again sometime. You can tell me all about Carleton in the old days. But we've come to collect Jack for lunch, and Pablo's hungry."

"Deirdre, why don't you join us?" Jack said. "We're going to the Faculty Club."

Jack is normally attuned to people's moods. He usually notices the slightest change in voice, body language, or facial expression. Not this time, or at least, not mine.

"I'd love to, Jack," she said, "but I have a committee meeting. Maybe we can get together later this afternoon. You know, catch up on old times. Are you still a tea drinker?"

He gestured at the stack of cardboard boxes on the floor. "I'll be here the rest of the day."

"Well, I have to get ready for that meeting. Good-bye, Anne. Nice to meet you. Good-bye, Pablo. I'll see you later, Jack." She strolled out the door.

Surprising she could walk in a skirt that tight.

Jack came over to kiss me.

I smelled her perfume. I offered my cheek.

Evidently his mood-detecting radar had switched back on. He changed the subject before I could start on it. "What do you think of the office?"

"It's big."

He drew me to the window. "How do you like the view?"

We looked over the La Jolla Farms Road residential area and west to the Pacific Ocean. The view was spectacular.

"Nice." I turned my back. "We'd better go."

"Anne —."

Pablo grabbed his hand and pulled him toward the door. "Abuelito, let's go!"

Jack shrugged and gestured for me to go ahead. He and Pablo followed.

Conversation at lunch was limited. Pablo did most of the talking.

When he and I left, I said to Jack, "Enjoy your tea."

*

That night, dinner was quiet.

Jack, who is Inuit, prefers to eat meat raw, and I've learned to do that, too, when we're in Ungavaq, our home in northern Québec. All that meat— ptarmigan, hare, seal, caribou, walrus, and even polar bear—is meat he's hunted himself. Away from Ungavaq, because we don't trust its cleanliness, we eat meat cooked rare. Tonight, I gave him an end slice of the roast beef.

Without comment, Jack ate everything I set before him.

*

After I cleaned the kitchen and put Pablo to bed, I said, "I think I'll go to bed early tonight."

Jack immediately rose. "Me too. First day on a new job is pretty tiring."

We walked to our room and silently busied ourselves with our ritual of preparations for bed. We folded the ice-blue bedspread, turned the sheet and blanket down, fluffed the pillows, and opened the windows.

Jack went to brush his teeth.

When he came out of the bathroom, I went in. There, I changed into the pink-sprigged flannel pajamas I'd taken from the chest of drawers.

I came out.

Jack sat in the bed with his pillows propped against the headboard. He'd pushed the blanket down because it was so warm. The sheet covered the lower half of his body. I could see the contours of his strong thighs. And even at sixty-two, his bare shoulders and arms were muscular and beautiful, his chest broad and smooth.

Jack isn't handsome by American standards. His hair, straight, coarse, and black with a few strands of gray, is brushed back from his face and reaches almost to his shoulders. Hazel eyes, inherited from his white grandfather, sit above a broad nose and high cheekbones.

Those eyes widened in surprise. "What are you wearing?"

"Pajamas."

"I didn't know you owned pajamas."

"I save them for nights when it's going to be *really cold*."

"Anne, don't be like that."

"Like what, dear?" I asked in my sunniest voice.

"She's just an old friend."

"An old friend." I nodded. "Yes, that looked like a *very friendly* kiss. Did you have your tongue in her mouth?"

"No, of course not," he said, his tone aggrieved, but his face a giveaway.

"Then, perhaps, did she have *her* tongue in *your* mouth?"

". . . Maybe a little."

"Right. 'Friendly.' I'm going to sleep now." I turned off my lamp, lay down, and turned my back to him. For the first time in the almost three years of our marriage, I didn't kiss him goodnight.

He slid down and adjusted his pillows. I heard the click as he turned off his light.

We lay in silence.

The bed shook as he moved toward me. He put his arm around me and slid his hand up under my pajama top. "Do you remember the first time I did this?"

"Yes."

I started to move away, but he caressed my breast and gently rolled the nipple with his thumb and forefinger. "And do you remember this?"

"Yes . . . Don't. It's hard to be angry when you do that."

"You want me to stop?"

". . . Yes."

He withdrew his hand. "Turn over."

"Why?"

"I want to show you how she kissed me, so you'll know it was just friendly."

I rolled over into his arms.

He kissed me the way he does. His tongue thrust into my mouth and he stroked and tantalized me until my toes curled.

"Is that the way she kissed you?" I asked when I had my breath back enough to talk.

"No. I didn't get that quite right. Let me try again."

He kissed me again.

"Was *that* the way?" I barely articulated.

"No." He shook his head. "Still not right."

And again.

"I really don't like these pajamas," he said. "I think you're going to be too warm."

"I think I'm already hot."

"Let me take them off you." He started unbuttoning the top.

Damn, it's hard to be mad at him.

*

I lay in his arms, relaxed, content.

He stroked my cheek gently. "I suppose I'd better tell you."

"That might be a good idea."

"She's the one I told you about before."

"Yes. Your mistress."

"No. Just the woman I slept with."

"Just."

"Yes, just."

"And you were just about to tell her you're married, as soon as she got her tongue out of your mouth?"

"Yes."

"What are you going to do now?"

"She's a colleague. I'll need to talk to her from time to time."

"No more kissing?"

He smiled. "No more kissing." He shook his head. He sighed.

"Although she does have a nice tongue."

I smacked him, and he laughed.

I snuggled into his arms.

The pajamas stayed on the floor, where they'd landed, until morning.

Candlelight

R. J. Black

If ever

I saw her

as the flame

on a candle,

it was

by grace

and not

my thick,

animal eyes.

The Minister and the Mafia

Harry Huntsman

My office door flew open. A bedraggled blonde lady said, "Reverend Huntsman, I've driven from Las Vegas this morning. My husband died there over the weekend. We were there for a little vacation and he died suddenly."

I must have looked as startled and puzzled as I felt. I waited. Occasionally someone having a delusional or psychotic episode came to see me unannounced.

"Oh, I'm Geri Williams."

Despite her anxious and rumpled appearance, I realized who she was, remembering how she looked when I last saw her.

"You helped me with the Wyatt family last year," I said.

She nodded.

Geri occasionally volunteered to investigate the needs of families that applied to churches for emergency food.

"You are the mother of Arthur and James."

"Yes," she said. "They would like you to conduct their father's funeral. I'll understand if you'd rather not. I'm sure you've heard the stories of his past, but that was a long time ago. He has been a stockbroker for years."

I had never met Geri's husband, Matt Williams, but had heard that he had been captain of a Mafia gambling boat off the

California coast in the 1930s, thirty years earlier. He had to be much older than Geri, mother of eighteen and twenty-five-year old sons.

"I'm sorry about your husband's death," I said.

Tears started again and I handed her a box of Kleenex.

"I'll be fine as soon as I get some rest and sleep."

Eighteen-year-old Arthur Williams had come to me for help in getting a morals waiver to be accepted in the Air Force. When he was fourteen he and a friend were caught stealing hubcaps for his brother, James, to sell. When James came to see me he said he had just completed training to be an insurance agent. He wanted to help me with youth work and he wanted me to sponsor him for membership in the Rotary Club. I had heard that while in the Marines in San Diego he had been charged with running drugs from Mexico to Los Angeles.

I wanted to ask Mrs. Williams about her husband's death in Las Vegas. There were frequent stories in the media, and several books, about gangsters killing associates or former associates. But after the shock of her husband's sudden death and the five- or six-hour drive across the California-Nevada desert, questions would have been cruel.

"Of course I'll conduct the service, Geri."

*

As I sat in the Clergy Room at the funeral chapel, the sound of recorded organ music surprised me. Neither the grieving widow nor I had mentioned asking my church organist to play for the funeral. Ordinarily, she was quick to volunteer. The two families lived on the same block. I was studying the list of pallbearers when the white-haired funeral director opened the door to the chapel and said, "It's time, Reverend." He seemed nervous, a rarity for funeral directors in my experience. They were more likely to help calm the minister.

A multi-generation crowd overflowed the chapel, unusual in my experience in California. Art Williams was in uniform, as were a number of his Air Force friends. There were so many young people present that I realized the brothers were much more popular than I thought due to their troubles with the law.

The large number of Geri's friends was less of a surprise. She was attractive, outgoing and caring. Apparently most of her friends came without their husbands. But there were about as many men as women in the crowd. I saw none of the Rotarians I had met in the five clubs of the Los Angeles harbor area.

I felt overwhelmed by the size of the crowd, and then I looked at the six pallbearers. I had never seen any them before. They sat on the front pew, much too close to the lectern. They wore expensive suits, diamonds in their watches, rings and tie pins. They stared at me with stony faces as the organ music wound down and I stepped to the lectern. Obviously they had not been consulted in the choice of clergy. I thought of stories I heard from fellow Rotarians after agreeing to conduct the funeral. Not only of the gambling boat days, but rumors that his stock brokerage was a front for the numbers gambling racket. However, I had never refused to conduct a funeral. Funerals are for the living.

After the sermon and viewing, the funeral director and I walked ahead of the casket and the six pallbearers to the hearse. As I stepped aside and glanced at the six old men, I remembered one of the first clichés I ever heard. "If looks could kill." The cemetery was twenty-five miles away. "Sir, may I ride with you?" The director's hands shook as he closed the rear doors of the hearse. "Of course, Reverend."

Half a dozen motorcycle escorts blocked traffic as the long funeral procession made its way to the freeway. I removed the funeral program from my pocket and asked, "Sir, do you know any of the pallbearers?"

"They are all from out of town, Reverend," the director said and focused intently on driving.

*

The Brown church, where I had been pastor three years, was in an unincorporated bed-room community of Los Angeles County. Built in 1928, it had become popular for weddings, often referred to simply as "the Brown church."

Sheriffs' deputies were our police. Captain Robert Weddle was commander of the nearest sheriff's station. We met at Rotary club meetings and become friends. He told me that his narcotics officers sometimes complained to him that they would be following a suspect and the suspect would disappear into my parsonage or church office. The day after the funeral I went to see him.

Captain Weddle's receptionist opened the door to his office. "Come in, Reverend!" His bass voice echoed. "How is your charm school?" The receptionist giggled behind me before closing the office door. So the captain's narcotics officers had been gossiping.

A few weeks earlier, I noticed a beautiful young woman with a three- or four-year-old child cruising local streets. The first time I noticed her she appeared to be having car trouble across the street from the church. Then I saw her in a local coffee shop at a table with five known drug pushers. She smiled when she saw that I noticed who she was with. She increased the frequency of her appearances, slowing her car and smiling suggestively as I walked between church and parsonage.

Two other sexy young women showed up, one even attended church services, attentive and friendly. The third would appear to be waiting for a ride at the intersection between church and parsonage. When the first beauty started parking beside the parsonage to fix her makeup, my wife called Captain Weddle. He sent Dixie, a narcotics detective, to interview us. He began investigating the women. The investigation grew to include five undercover narcotics officers.

Their findings surprised the police and shocked my wife and me. Detective Dixie said the three beauties were wives or girlfriends of drug dealers who were angry at my drug counseling, lectures and newspaper articles about the drug epidemic. They were especially angry at my going to juvenile court with and counseling young drug offenders and their parents. The biggest shock to all of us was that four drug gangs from our bedroom community of 8,000 residents were the primary suppliers of drugs to five surrounding cities.

I was so embarrassed my face burned. "Charm school, just what my marriage needs right now," I said. "It's not very flattering to learn that the women who flirt with you are being paid or ordered to do it."

He was still laughing at my embarrassment when I handed him the program from the Williams funeral. "Do you recognize the names of any of these pallbearers?"

Suddenly his face was red. His entire demeanor changed. He leaned over his desk and yelled "You mean Meyer Lansky was in my county and you didn't call me?"

"Who is Meyer Lansky?" I asked.

"Oh, my God!" The captain groaned. He laid his head on his arms on his desk. After a minute or so he raised his head and said, "Meyer Lansky is America's top gangster." He buzzed the receptionist. "Send Lieutenant Brizzlow in here." A door opened and a tall man in expensive civilian clothes came in.

"Lieutenant Brizzlow, this is Reverend Huntsman." I shook hands with the officer. The captain handed him the list of pallbearers. "This country preacher has no idea what he has gotten into in the big city." The captain knew I had been student pastor of rural churches in Arkansas and Texas.

To me he said, "Lieutenant Brizzlow specializes in organized crime.

"Lieutenant, show the preacher these pallbearers in our mug books."

A different Type of Underage Drinking

Joe Naiman

In the early 1980s, the legal drinking age of 21 wasn't enforced as rigorously as it is now, so from 1981 until I turned 21 in January 1985, I was pretty successful in my efforts to obtain alcoholic beverages.

I first got away with drinking in a bar when I was 17.

In 1981, Ron Zappardino, who was originally from Philadelphia, owned a bar in Downtown San Diego called Frenchy Marseilles. Ron also had an entity called the Philadelphia Club— for San Diegans who once lived in Philadelphia. Between when I was seven months old and when I was two, the Army stationed my father at Fort Valley Forge Hospital and we lived in the Philadelphia suburb of Phoenixville, so, even though I was young at the time and lived in a suburb, Ron let me join The Philadelphia Club.

In fall 1981, The Philadelphia Eagles were on Monday Night Football and Ron held a Philadelphia Club event at Frenchy Marseilles. Kamikazes were $1. The Eagles scored early in the game and, at age 17, I gave the bartender my dollar and was served. If I hung around the right company I could buy liquor after that.

My grandparents' 50th anniversary celebration in March 1982 included an open bar. I was 18 and my brother Martin was 13. I asked the bartender for a kamikaze and he gave me one. When Martin found out what it was, he asked for one. He was turned down, and that was the end of my liquor at the open bar, too. However, during dinner I was seated at a table with wine. No one was watching, but I refrained anyway.

When I enrolled at Northwestern University, the drinking age in Wisconsin was 18 at the time, and a few days after my 19th birthday I had my first legal drink. Freshmen weren't allowed to have cars on campus, which meant I could drink all I wanted without worrying about driving drunk.

Our dorm went on a ski trip to Lake Geneva, and after I failed to master the bunny slope I retired to the lodge. I ordered a kamikaze and was given one, along with a quote for $2.50. I paid the money and drank my kamikaze. It was that simple; there wasn't the challenge of getting away with drinking because I was too young.

My 21st birthday had no big significance. My first alcoholic drink after I turned 21 was a glass of wine in a Persian restaurant in Chicago. Drinking or buying alcohol was suddenly without the excitement of trying to beat the drinking age.

Between my first drink in a bar and the time I turned 21, I got carded twice: once at a topless bar in the company of an older friend and once at the Northwestern Student Bar when I was with an older co-worker who wanted to continue our conversation.

In both cases it was the other person rather than myself who wanted to go to the bar, so getting carded and denied was more a matter of principle. Now, getting carded is once again a matter of principle; if I look young enough to attract a 20-year-old woman I'm going to take my winnings and go home.

Forward to 2013. Jack in the Box had a $1.99 Ultimate Cheeseburger special. That, a value drink, and sales tax in unincorporated San Diego County translated into a $3.23 meal. I had taken advantage of that special enough times to know what I owed before I ordered.

One afternoon in May, the cashier told me that my order came to $2.69. I figured she might have omitted an item. Then she gave me my receipt. I had ordered a value drink, but she gave me the senior drink price. At 49, I had automatically received my first 55-and-over senior discount!

So far that's been the only time I got away with the senior drink discount while being underage. Between now and when I turn 55 in January, 2019, we'll see anyone else gives me a senior discount when I'm actually too young to qualify.

Kalawao

Chloe Edge

In the forest above Father Damien's Leper Colony on the island of Molokai, in Hawaii, there is a lot going on. Trees are growing, trade winds blow, birds come and go, but that is not what I mean. This place is crowded with spirits. At first I couldn't believe it. What used to be Father Damien's Leper Colony is now a tourist attraction.

Below the waist-high, cold, stone wall is a sharp cliff and at the bottom of that is the old leper colony. People who had been diagnosed with leprosy had been removed from their homes by state authorities and brought to live out their lives here. This is a flat area of land surrounded on all but one side by treacherous, shark-filled ocean and the one side has a steep rocky cliff behind it. It would be virtually impossible to climb this sheer black rock, even for a goat. I'm at the top of the cliff trying to understand way too much at once.

We had followed a well-worn path from the parking area, walked into the pine forest about fifteen minutes. No one else is around because it's early. Besides, it's Molokai and hardly anyone comes here anyway. It's foggy and cool. The dark-green pine trees smell dewy-fresh and dried brown pine needles crunch under our feet. The salt smell of the sea goes straight up my nose and into my head. I can hear the ocean thundering not too far away and it doesn't sound like any place you'd go for a picnic.

We are looking for a specific large rock that is supposed to look like a huge penis in the middle of the forest. Naturally, I'm curious. We find the big rock, in the middle of a clearing, and it does, in fact, look like they say. While we are wondering how it got there I notice through the misty air some roundish shapes, white-grayish, hovering in midair, barely moving, but never completely still. Odd, I thought, and I moved around a little to see them in a different light. Then I noticed more of them. Spirits. Some bigger than others. Entities. Bold, I thought — they're letting me see them.

I asked my husband and son (who don't believe in any of this kind of stuff) if they could see them. They could. Amazing.

We are on a small island, standing on a mountain in a clearing of a pine forest, next to a 10-foot-long penis, jutting not straight out of the earth but at an angle, surrounded by opaque shapes, sort of circular, which, when I move toward them, are not there anymore. They are so clear, I am sure they will show up on film, so I take some photos. I do not even realize that I am observing something I will never forget.

I decide to go back to the stone wall, have another look down at the leper colony of Kalawao, read a few signs put up for the tourists. Maybe these misty circles will be gone when the fog clears a little. Everything is down there, a little church, some dormitories, a hospital, a store, cafeteria, grassy areas — this is a compound from which no one escaped. In 1873, Father Damien, the Belgian Roman Catholic missionary, began his work on the Kalaupapa Peninsula of North Molokai. Everyone who went there, died there, including Father Damien. Now they call leprosy Hansen's Disease, and they have a cure for it. People don't have to be quarantined anymore.

I've read stories about a man named Koolau, from Kauai, who was in love with his wife. They had a son. When he was diagnosed with leprosy, he knew he'd be captured and transported to the leper colony. He took his wife and son to the Kalalau Valley on the NaPali coast, a remote area on the North Shore of Kauai, accessible only by sea or by a difficult 13-hour hike. They lived there until the sheriff found him and killed him because he refused to be captured and taken to the leper colony on Molokai.

I feel so sad. I can taste the salt from this dangerous ocean. Lots of people didn't want to come here to live and to die away from their families. If courage had a flavor, I could taste it, too.

I turn away from the pounding ocean surrounding the compound and walk back into the forest. The air is cool and wet and clean and there is so much I do not understand. The roundish shapes are still there, lots of them, sort of hovering around, hanging out here in the forest. I am not afraid. Soon we have to leave.

At the Molokai Airport, we board a Hawaiian Air plane to return to Kauai. I keep thinking about what I've seen in the forest. When we land, I look for my camera in my backpack and it isn't there. I search my luggage. Nowhere is my camera. Frantic, I report my missing camera and they search the plane. Nothing.

Back on the mainland, in Escondido, I've resigned myself to my loss and go to a little appliance store, A-1 Appliance, on Escondido Boulevard to replace my camera. The woman working there is from Hawaii. Distraught, I tell her the story I just told you. She says, "You cannot take photos of spirits. They took your camera!"

First Lady Never Perspires — Never

Ellen Shaw Tufts

---Originally published March 10, 1980 as a feature for the *Green Bay News-Chronicle*

5:05 p.m., March 9, 1980. Austin Straubel Airport, Green Bay, WI — United States First Lady Rosalynn Carter arrives at Executive Air Service Terminal on a flight from the Milwaukee County Airport. No matter if you're a Secret Service agent or a local TV crew member, it's apparently helpful to wear a tiny plastic earphone while covering the First Lady's meanderings through the crowd. Rosalynn appears cool, with every moment calculated and poised, as she steps down from the DC-6, flanked by a few personal aides and Secret Service agents. She does not communicate, she does not wave. What she does is almost smile.

5:12 p.m. The F.L. proceeds to the press area for a few brief comments as photo crew starts shooting. "Hey, dammit, you're in the picture," says a WBAY/TV 2 cameraman, growling to a reporter. "Move it, O.K.?" Rosalynn and her personal secretary walk towards the podium, both wearing capes as the chilling southwest March wind from the Fox River whips around. On her right is former Wisconsin Governor Martin Schreiber, a prominent

Democrat on hand for this fund-raiser benefiting the state's Eighth Congressional District. He explains how President Jimmy Carter will join the group at about 8 p.m., flying in from Milwaukee, and adds that Rosalynn is happy to be in Wisconsin.

5:17 p.m. The First Lady tells the crowd that OPEC oil prices are hoisting up inflation on the national scene. "One thing," she comments softly, "is how slowly Congress moves — the windfall profits tax finally was passed this week."

5:40 p.m. Rosalynn departs from Executive Air Service Terminal in a limousine en route to Riverside Ballroom, followed by several official cars, and a WBAY-TV 2 news truck; the procession is quiet, orderly.

6:05 p.m. She proceeds to the Riverside Ballroom main banquet room for the dinner. On stage, a musical trio composed of Green Bay Symphony concertmaster Isadore Mednikow on the violin, local pianist Sadie Jerry, and cellist Carol Stanel perform with charming schmaltz numbers such as "People Will Say We're in Love," "When I Marry Mister Snow," and a passionate rendition of "Jealousy," as a crowd of several hundred enters the ballroom. In a flanked area, the press munches on fried chicken, carrot sticks, brownies and Rice Krispies bars with coffee and soft drinks on the side."Where's Rosalynn?" asks someone. "This is her private time," answers a national TV crew member. "I've been covering the Carters since '76—Rosalynn takes her time. This First Lady never perspires," he adds. "Never."

6:17 p.m. Out in the hall, the crowd sits down at long banquet tables while the food is brought in, mainly steaming platters of fried chicken, mashed potatoes, cranberry sauce, cold slaw, rolls and squishy, gooey desserts. From the stage comes a chorus of "Can't Help Loving Dat Man..."

6:22 p.m. The cool, poised First Lady walks down the aisle and sits at the dais, surrounded by Governor Schreiber, Eighth District Chairman Sam Halloin and Green Bay Mayoral Assistant Paul Willems. She gives a slight wave as the crowd, still awaiting President Jimmy Carter, digs into mashed potatoes and the trio plays "Happy Days Are Here Again."

Good Sports

Joe Naiman

I grew up in San Diego and have lived in the San Diego area since I was two years old, with the exception of some college years. Those college quarters were spent at Northwestern University in Evanston, Illinois, which is just north of Chicago.

There are considerable differences between San Diego and Chicago, and during my senior year in 1984 one significant difference was baseball loyalties.

Once I arrived in the northern suburbs of Chicago, I rooted for the Cubs for 150 games a year. At the time, teams played 12 games during the season against opponents from another division, and when the Padres played the Cubs my baseball heritage contrasted with the mainstream of Wrigleyville. The situation intensified during the 1984 season, when the Padres won the division for the first time ever and the Cubs finished in first place for the first time in my lifetime. The two teams squared off in the National League playoff series.

Cubs fans respect loyalty. They treated me better than those who hadn't cared for the Cubs when they were in fifth or sixth place and suddenly joined the bandwagon. They weren't pleased with what happened during that playoff, when the Padres came down from a two-game deficit to take the final three games and the series, but they never faulted me for rooting for the Padres.

I still had to celebrate alone. Since McDonald's owner and founder Ray Kroc bought the Padres in 1974 and since his widow owned the Padres at the time, a local McDonald's was the most appropriate place to celebrate. One of those billions of burgers McDonald's has served was a celebratory meal that night.

So when the Padres lost the World Series a week later to the Detroit Tigers, who at the time were owned by the founder and owner of Domino's Pizza, the sportsmanlike thing to do was to have dinner that night at an area Domino's. My friend Rob, who was raised a Baltimore Orioles fan, also considered this appropriate, so Rob and I set out for the nearest Domino's.

The Domino's in Evanston was scheduled to open soon, which wouldn't be soon enough to dine there the night the Tigers won the world championship. The phone book was the proper solution.

There were just a couple of problems. The phone book listing for Domino's was 650 ANNW Hwy in Des Plaines. The ANNW was a foreign term to me.

The other problem was that the final game of the 1984 World Series wasn't the only significant event for me that day. I had started the school year in a lounge while waiting for a dormitory room to open. Earlier that day I was notified of the opportunity to move into an actual room in Courtyard Hall, which is part of

Northwestern University the way Alaska is part of the United States—it's a campus dorm, but Courtyard and the athletic complex across the street are three-quarters of a mile from anywhere else on campus and about a mile and a half from most of the academic buildings. Since I brought my car with me that year, I accepted the offer to move to Courtyard. The following day I would make arrangements with Illinois Bell for phone service.

The lack of a phone prevented me from calling that Domino's and finding out exactly what ANNW Hwy meant. At least Rob and I knew that it was in Des Plaines, so we headed in that direction. We soon realized that the NW probably meant that the Domino's was on Northwest Highway. Eventually we figured out that 650 ANNW Hwy meant Suite A of 650 North Northwest Highway. That meant finding the Domino's was now merely a matter of following the street numbers.

Although the Domino's closed earlier on Sundays than on Fridays and Saturdays, Rob and I arrived less than an hour before it closed. We ordered our pizza and ate it in my car. The Detroit Tigers' victory in the 1984 World Series was properly celebrated with appropriate sportsmanship.

And getting back to campus was much easier than the trip to the Domino's.

The 1969 Chevrolet Impala

Fred Crothers

My father died in 1978 and left my mom a beautiful 1969 Chevrolet Impala. She decided to get her driver's license soon after he died so that the car would not stand idle. She always took very good care of it and had it serviced regularly at the local Chevrolet dealer. My Blazer was in the shop for a tune-up so I asked her to lend me the Chevy for a few days. She was such a sweetheart, she just said "fine." I had my wife, Dawn, drop me off at my mom's house and I drove the Chevy to our home in Carson, just twenty-five miles down the river. Her car was immaculate, so I drove it very carefully and only used it for short trips. It was parked directly in front of my house on a side street off the Wind River Highway, next door to the tavern.

That evening I was tending bar and it was relatively quiet. Avery was the only one who was doing any serious drinking. Earlier he had a fight with his wife, Patti, and she left in a huff and drove home by herself. Avery was a truck driver for a local outfit called Ober Logging. He was short and stocky with blond curly hair cut close to the scalp, and though he spoke with a gruff voice he was affable for the most part. He drank a lot that evening, but never seemed out of control. His pickup was parked directly across the highway from the tavern door, headed downhill on the far side of the road. He only needed to make a U-turn and drive a short distance to his home.

It was about eleven when he got off his stool and headed out the door. He moseyed across the highway, opened the door and clambered into his pickup. Several minutes passed as I waited for him to start it up, and finally he turned on the headlights. As I watched through the window he rolled down the hill, made a wide swing to the left and crashed his pickup directly into the left front fender of my mom's car!

I called the sheriff's office and one of the deputies responded within moments. We approached the truck, only to find Avery fast asleep at the wheel. I was so glad that the deputy was there and was smart enough to take a couple of Polaroid pictures. He didn't want to arrest Avery, so I called his wife and she drove down to the tavern right away. When she arrived, the deputy helped her shove Avery over so that Patti could drive him home in the pickup.

I called Avery the next morning and asked him how he wanted to handle the damage. He was angry and denied the whole incident. He did not recall the accident or even being at the bar. Thank goodness his wife, Patti, had showed up to drive him home and that the deputy snapped a picture of him asleep at the wheel and another showing his pickup slammed into my mother's car. I told him exactly what happened and told him I would get estimates for the repairs.

I checked with several garages and they said it would cost about $600, and they were very concerned about ever matching the metallic grey paint. One of the repairmen from the garage suggested that I check with a wrecking yard to see if I could get a fender from a wrecked car and save several weeks of waiting for the body shop to find one. I called a friend of mine from White Salmon who had a wrecking yard. He said that he did have a couple of '69 Chevy's at his yard and told me to come over and check them out.

I drove my mom's car out to his wrecking yard on a dusty old wagon road, hoping that I would not get high-centered on the heavy growth in between the ruts. I met with my friend Al and he told me which row to check out. I looked and sure enough, there were two '69 Chevys side by side. They were both very badly mangled, but one of them did have the left front fender intact, including the headlamp. It was a perfect match for my mother's car! The fender was the identical color, a metallic gray. I talked to Al and asked him if he had someone who could make the swap for me? He said that Max, a guy that worked for him at the yard, would remove the damaged fender and replace it for me. It fit just like the original; what a miracle! I paid $100 for the fender and $50 to Max for his good work. I drove the Impala home and spent the afternoon waxing and buffing it until the whole car shone like new again.

I called Avery and explained how I was able to get the car

fixed so quickly, and he too was amazed and glad that it could be remedied so quickly. He brought me a check for the damage and it was over. I returned the car to my mother and never said another word about it to anyone.

Bosnia, 1997

a reflection

Anne Hoiberg

Bullet-pocked, smoke-shrouded homes, deserted buildings.

Untilled fields display danger signs of land mines.

Small villages emptied of life in Bosnia's abandoned war zone.

Refugees as their homes looted, then torched.

Ragged human remnants of 1990s war, land of pervasive sadness.

Together, talking of hatred and killings, seeking hope.

Deadly devastation and futility of war —

Once Bosnia, now Afghanistan, Iraq, Gaza, Pakistan, Syria,

Ukraine . . .

CONTRIBUTORS

Diana Avery Amsden, Ph. D. — Diana's academic background is largely anthropology, archaeology, architecture, and art history. Googling her name reveals she has written scholarly and popular works, an index to Ayn Rand's *Atlas Shrugged*, and poems and a short story in the 2013 *The Guilded Pen*. Soon to be published is the first volume of *The Stained Glass Woman*, a multigenerational family story. Imagine *The Forsythe Saga* in coastal California, Santa Fe, and Berkshires. Her editor is Mark Clements and Karla Olson, advisor. www.DianaAmsden.com.

Simone Arias, Ph.D. — Simone's storytelling began in high school as feature editor of the high school newspaper and evolved into a job as radio reporter in Los Angeles. Writing skills then were transformed into teaching high school journalism, English, drama, and social studies. Most of her published articles have focused on teaching humanities which currently involves linking San Diego to American and world history curriculum for teachers and college professors. She is a board member of the San Diego Writer/Editors Guild and holds the office of Secretary. She is the poetry editor for *The Guilded Pen, Third Edition*. Simone is active in volunteering opportunities to encourage writing for everyone — from curious children to seasoned citizens.

Gered Beeby — Gered is Past President (2003) of the San Diego Writers/Editors Guild and remains on the Board as a Director-At-Large ("Official Greeter"). His suspense/thriller novel of industrial espionage, *Dark Option* (2002) was nominated for a PMA Benjamin Franklin award in the category, Best New Voice – Fiction (2003). He has also written *Dark Option* for the screen. Gered's screenplay, "The Bottle Imp," is a deal-with-the-devil tale based on Robert Louis Stevenson's 1892 classic. His work also appears in *The Guilded Pen* (2012 and 2013). Gered continues to work on screenplays, is writing his memoirs, and serves as a reviewer for the San Diego Book Awards.

R.J. Black — R.J. was born and raised in Mexico City. He was educated in Massachusetts and California. After working on both sides of the U.S.-Mexico border for thirty years, he retired in Coronado to live with his girlfriend and write an historical novel about the Mexican War. In between chapters, he works in real-estate, body surfs and writes poetry. He has published in several student magazines and small presses, including *Red, City Beat, San Diego Poetry* and *The Guilded Pen* (2012). The highlight of his year was driving from San Diego to Chicago with his daughter in a red 2014 Chevy Traverse.

Joseph Bonpensiero (Lt. Col., USAF Ret.) — Joe's San Diego roots inspired him to write his first memoir about his youth at sea with his commercial fisherman father entitled *Chocolate Moon* (2012*)*. In 2014 he will publish *NIPUTI...the Nephew* — an exposé about Frank Bompensiero, his uncle, a Mafia Don and one of California's most feared killers. Joe is currently working on *Just My Shorts* — an anthology of short stories and poems. He has also begun a memoir of his Vietnam War experiences, *Dinner in Happy Valley*. Joe was published in *The Guilded Pen* (2012) and (2013).

Marcia Buompensiero — Writer and editor of *The Guilded Pen, Second* and *Third Editions*, Marcia is the author of the Theo Hunter mystery series: *Dirty Little Murders* (2009), *Deadly Little Secrets* (2014) and *Fatal Little Lies* (summer of 2015). *Deadly Little Secrets* received a "highly recommended" rating from the SDW/EG Manuscript Review Board. She was published in *The Guilded Pen* (2013). Her nonfiction work has appeared in *The Southern Cross*, the San Diego Diocesan newspaper. Marcia is a board member of the San Diego Writers/Editors Guild and holds the office of Treasurer.

John Cain — John is a musician, composer, author, teacher, orchestrator, conductor and bandleader. He plays piano, guitar, bass, harmonica and accordion, and sings in five languages. In addition to live performances he gives educational seminars on the history of jazz, Latin music, and classical music. He is an Artist in Residence with the Southern California Jazz Society and a Docent with the Advocates For Classical Music in affiliation with the San Diego Symphony. He is author of the book *Life's A Good Gig*, nominated for best non-fiction book by the San Diego Book & Writers Awards, 2008. Websites: www.johncain.info and www.lifesagoodgig.com.

Lawrence Richard Carleton — Larry has published and presented scholarly work in philosophy, cognitive science, and software development, thereby putting to use his advanced degrees in computer science and philosophy and his post-doctorate in cognitive science. In recent years, he has turned to short story writing. Larry is alarmed at the tendency in some to enforce intolerance toward those who question beliefs which are false and harmful. He believes if a belief gets bruised when it bumps up against reality, it is the belief, not the reality, which needs adjustment. Larry's short stories attempt to prompt interest in unfamiliar points of view — an exercise in promoting the acceptance or, at least tolerance, of diversity in responsible thought. His short stories have been published in *The Guilded Pen* (2012 and 2013).

Anne Casey — Anne has edited three newsletters, including that of the Sharp Memorial Hospital Women's Auxiliary. She studied Literature and Writing at the University of California, San Diego. Her poetry has been published in *The Guilded Pen* (2012 and 2013). Anne is a former SDW/EG board member. She writes poetry, short fiction and creative non-fiction and has two non-fiction books in progress.

Bradley Collins — Brad is an elementary school teacher who enjoys teaching writing to his primary grade students. As a successful grant writer, Brad helped improve his school with a Life Sciences Center. Brad also enjoys entering fiction and science fiction stories into writing contests, and composing lyric videos collaboratively with his students on YouTube. Currently he is developing a few different children's book ideas with a talented art teacher and finishing his first young adult fictional novel, which has recently been recommended by the SDW/EG Manuscript Review Program.

Alan Converse — Al started writing Vietnam War press releases as a young naval officer, earning him recognition in the Pacific Fleet. After active duty in the Navy and earning his MBA, he entered the field of banking and later, government lending with the Small Business Administration. He has published two novels, *Bitch'n* (2012) and *Die Again*. His short stories have appeared in previous issues of The Guilded Pen: "Warrior's Stone" (2012) and "The Marble Game" (2013). Al is a John D. MacDonald fan, likes to read *Scientific American* and *The Economist* and hopes someday the San Diego Chargers will win the Super Bowl or the playoffs, or the Division, or something — please!

Margaret Coughlin — Margaret is happily retired and enjoys seeing how words can express actions and emotions. Although she has had several travel articles published, she prefers to write short fiction and been supported by the writers in OASIS classes. She was published in *The Guilded Pen* (2012 and 2013). Recently, she has published a collection of short stories in the fantasy genre.

Barbara Crothers — Barbara and her husband Fred fell in love with Mexico and its people during their many trips south of the border. On hiatus for two years, 1989-1991, they traveled through all of its states and Guatemala. She kept journals while visiting great cities, small villages, and meeting people along the way. Barbara is writing stories about those souls they met in out-of-the-way places. She was published in *The Guilded Pen* (2012 and 2013). Barbara previously served on the SDW/EG board of directors for four years and held the office of Secretary for two years.

Fred Crothers — Fred is currently editing a book of short stories based on lumberjacks and other rascals who wandered in and out of his life while he owned and operated a small tavern near the Columbia River in the forested Pacific Northwest. He was published in *The Guilded Pen* (2012 and 2013).

John Davis — John is a U.S. Army veteran who served in Vietnam and has since earned degrees and worked in various contractor positions, including in Afghanistan and Kuwait and with the U.S. Navy. He found time to foster his writing skills by submitting articles to professional publications and travel magazines. He has published seven journal articles and a book on federal contracting, as well as a publication in the *Proceedings of the Society of Logistics Engineers*. John is a member of the ABA, the Black Tie Club International, Great Books Reading Club. He is a Life Member and a past president of the SDW/EG.

Marie DiMercurio – Marie is working on her first writing venture, *From Birth Until Sunset – Poisoned to Death*. She is dedicated to sharing her experiences and what she has learned about the dangers of the standard American diet. Marie's essay on "Life's Lessons" appears in this issue of *The Guilded Pen* (2014).

Bob Doublebower — Bob was born in Philadelphia and raised in the southern New Jersey town of Lindenwold. He attended Villanova University, where he received a Bachelor's Degree in Civil Engineering. He began his engineering work with Bechtel Power division in Washington, D.C. His career has taken him to Colorado, Arizona, Virginia and California. He now maintains a consulting engineering practice, Regional Shorting Design, in San Diego county. He was published in *The Guilded Pen* (2012 and 2013) and is currently working on a horror novel, *The Circling Bench*. Bob is a past-president of SDW/EG and currently serves as Vice President on the board of directors.

Chloe K. Edge — Chloe holds a degree in Lit/Writing from UCSD. She published *Birdcage Review* (1982) and *Maize, Vol. 6* (1983). *Tattoo* (1988), was published for women in prison to celebrate seven years free from drugs, alcohol and incarceration. Chloe was also published in *The Guilded Pen* (2012 and 2013). She writes poems, nonfiction, and is currently working on a memoir.

David Feldman — Dave spent 30 years as copy editor at *The San Diego Union-Tribune*, 55 years working as a reporter and editor on newspapers, including *Stars & Stripes* in Europe and *Honolulu Star-Bulletin*. He has taught journalism in colleges for 34 years. Dave was published in *The Guilded Pen* (2012 and 2013) and tirelessly copyedited the 2013 and 2014 editions. Dave is semi-retired and still accepts editing assignments when he's not tinkering with classic cars.

Anne Hoiberg — Anne is president of the Women's Museum of California and a retired research psychologist who has published two books and more than 130 scientific articles, book chapters, reports, and presentations. She writes and speaks on women's and girls' rights, trafficking in women and children, women's political participation, United Nations, the status of women in Iraq, Afghanistan, Cuba, and the Middle East, and world peace.

Lisa Hunt—Lisa published *One Salute Too Many* (2013), which is used for post-traumatic stress disorder patients with Sherri's Wounded Warrior Project and the Veterans Administration, Escondido. She has also published a children's book, *Lizard In Grandma's Pants* (2014), which has sold in England as well as in the United States, and was recently purchased for the Hage Elementary School in Mira Mesa.

Harry Huntsman—Harry was born on a farm in Arkansas in 1925, the oldest of nine children. None of his family, neighbors or Sunday school teachers had more than an eight-grade education. After fifteen years as a minister in Arkansas, Texas and California, he taught middle and high school twelve years. Harry is at work on a novel about the Tennessee River and the Civil War, and a memoir, *A Pastor in Three States*. He was published in *The Guilded Pen* (2012 and 2013). Harry is a member of the SDW/EG board of directors and holds the office of President.

Carolyn Jaynes, M.A.—Carolyn's second book, *Poetic Lessons* (2014), is a collection of poignant poems, some of which appear in context in her inspirational book of true miracle stories, *Sprinkles from Heaven – Stories of Serendipity* (2014), available on Amazon.com. Carolyn has an M.A. from National University in Counseling Psychology, and has entertained thousands as a professional singer. As a former educator, social worker, and therapist, she realized she might uplift, inform, and inspire even more people with her books. Carolyn was published in *The Guilded Pen* (2012 and 2013) and lives in San Diego, California, where she roller-skates at the beach, flirts with hummingbirds, and grows cucumbers.

Richard Lederer, Ph.D. — Recipient of an "Odin Award" for his contributions to the writing arts in San Diego, as well as multiple San Diego Book Awards, Richard is the author of more than 40 books about language, history, and humor, including his best-selling *Anguished English* series and his current books, *Amazing Words, Monsters Unchained!,* and the *American Trivia Quiz Book.* Dr. Lederer's syndicated column, "Lederer on Language," appears in newspapers and magazines throughout the United States, including the San Diego *Union-Tribune*, and he is a founding co-host of "A Way With Words" on KPBS Public Radio. He has been named International Punster of the Year and Toastmasters International's Golden Gavel winner.

Ruth Leyse-Wallace, Ph.D., RD — Ruth has published two books on the links between nutrition and mental health since retiring from clinical practice in dietetics. She is a frequent contributor to the newsletter of the Behavioral Health Nutrition practice group and was published in *The Guilded Pen* (2012 and 2013). Ruth is past president of SDW/EG, serves on the board of directors, and is the Editor of *The Writer's Life,* the monthly newsletter of SDW/EG. She enjoys traveling, and especially likes to read books on consciousness and spirituality.

Caroline McCullagh — Caroline has lived most of her life in San Diego County. She earned a master's degree in cultural anthropology from UCSD. She has written four novels, with a fifth in progress, featuring the characters in her short story. She edited a cookbook, *Sing for Your Supper*, for San Diego Opera, and helped write and perform *The Singing Mirror*, a short opera. She also writes book reviews for the San Diego Horticultural Society (for twelve years). With her writing partner, Richard Lederer, she has written *American Trivia: What We All Should Know About U.S. History, Culture & Geography* (2012), the *American Trivia Quiz Book* (2014), and was published in *The Guilded Pen* (2013). Caroline and Richard also write an ongoing column on American history for the San Diego Union-Tribune.

Joe Naiman — Joe is a freelance writer and the co-author of the baseball history book, *The San Diego Padres Encyclopedia* (2002), and is the author of *The School with All the Catchers* (2012), a history of the Crawford H.S. baseball program. He is also the author of a novel, *Another Chance* (2006), and was published in *The Guilded Pen* (2012 and 2013). Joe has been a member of the Society for American Baseball Research since 1980 and was the coordinator of SABR's 1993 national convention in San Diego.

Richard Peterson — Rick has written magazine articles and was a former staff writer for *Wholistic Living News*. He authored the article, "Stained Glass Television," in the *Journal of Popular Culture* (Vol. 19. No. 4); a chapter called "Electric Sisters" in the *God Pumpers: Religion in the Electronic Age* (Bowling Green State University Popular Press), and was published in *The Guilded Pen* (2012 and 2013) . He is working on a sci-fi suspense thriller. Rick serves on the SDW/EG board of directors as Membership Chairman.

Ty Piz — Ty raced Motocross and Flatrack from 1972 through 1979. In 1980 he switched to road racing until retiring in 2004. He has won three regional championships and twice finished Top Ten overall in the AMA Superbike Series onboard a Yamaha TZ-250 Grand Prix motorcycle. Ty is an instructor for Total Control Advanced Rider Courses and coaches youth soccer camps. He was published in *The Guilded Pen* (2012 and 2013).

Norma Posy — After a lengthy career as a civilian scientist for the U.S. Navy designing submarine sonar systems, Norma retired in 2006 and published *Norma's Voice* (P.D. Publishing, 2006) which took first prize in the annual San Diego Book Awards. *Side Pocket*, recently released for Kindle, is a 73,000-word contemporary adventure/murder novel. www.norma-posy.com

Phil Pryde—San Diego State University Professor Emeritus Phil Pryde has authored several non-fiction books published by Cambridge University Press, Wiley Interscience, Westview Press, and Kendall-Hunt, the best know of which is, *Conservation in the Soviet Union* (Cambridge, 1972). He has authored over a hundred published academic papers. The revised 5th edition of his *San Diego: An Introduction to the Region* appeared in September 2014. Phil is optimistically working on his first fiction manuscript.

Alan Russell— Alan is the bestselling author of ten novels: *No Sign of Murder* (1990), *The Forest Prime Evil* (1992), *The Hotel Detective* (1994), *The Fat Innkeeper* (1995), *Multiple Wounds* (1996), *Shame* (1998), *Exposure* (2002), *Political Suicide* (2003), *Burning Man* (2012) and *St. Nick* (2013). His eleventh novel, *Guardians of the Night*, will be published on January 1, 2015. He is the recipient of numerous awards: The Lefty Award, 1996 (*The Fat Innkeeper*), USA's Today Critic's Choice Award, 1995/1996 (*The Fat Innkeeper*), Anthony Award nominee for best novel of the year, 1997 (*Multiple Wounds*), Macavity Award nominee for best novel of the year, 1997 (*Multiple Wounds*). For more information about Alan, go to his website www.alanrussell.net, or "like" him on Facebook: www.facebook.com/AlanRussellMysteryAuthor.

Mardie Schroeder—She has been a member of a writing group for two years. Mardie has participated in the SDW/EG "Open-Mic Night" as a reader of her short stories. She recently completed a romance novella titled *A Silent Man* and has begun work on a second novella. Mardie's short stories "Sudden Death" and "The Watering Hole" appear in this year's edition of *The Guilded Pen* (2014).

Charlotte Thompson, M.D. — is the author of eight books. She is published by William Morrow, Random House, Oxford University Press, Econ-Verlag in Germany and Jessica Kingsley Publisher in the UK and U.S. Her first book, *Raising a Handicapped Child*, first published by William Morrow in 1986, still sells now in its fifth edition. *Grandparenting a Child with Special Needs* (Jessica Kingsley Publisher 2009) is her latest book. Four other books are completed and currently being reviewed by different publishers. www.drthompsonsbooks.com.

Ellen Shaw Tufts — Ellen worked as assistant copyeditor at *House Beautiful Magazine* (Hearst Magazines) in New York City. Awards include the Wisconsin United Press International (UPI) award for excellence in column writing (1982) at the Green Bay News-Chronicle. She served as the San Diego National Council on Alcoholism-Drug Dependence (NCADD) news editor, earning her the Markie Award as newsletter editor. She is a former member, Society of Professional Journalists (national and local chapters), and is a correspondent and freelance writer of nonfiction. Ellen was published in *The Guilded Pen* (2012) and is a member of the SDW/EG board of directors.

Sam Warren — Sam's writing and publishing career began in the '60's while an Army Sergeant stationed in Moscow where he was a part-time editor of the embassy newsletter. He has published a number of tabloids including the *Santa Ana Journal*, the *Uptown San Diego Examiner,* and the *Border Business Journal*. He has also published: *Having Fun in Tijuana* (1988), *Tales from the Tijuana Jails* (2008), and the *Bible Naked* (2011). Sam is the publisher/editor of SDWriteWay.org, a Webzine for readers and writers, and is a publishing consultant and book and eBook formatter. Sam was published in *The Guilded Pen* (2012) and is a past president of the SDW/EG (2010-2011).

Wayne T. Williams, Ph.D. — After being expunged from California State University in 1970 by Ronald Reagan's mandate, along with many other anti-Vietnam war protestors and environmentalists, Wayne sought refuge for three years on a wilderness ranch in San Luis Obispo County. That break from politics permitted him time to publish numerous poems, essays and short stories. Since Wayne was blacklisted, the only academic work he could find was in Guatemala. That led to sixteen years of developmental work with USAID in Latin America and then eastern Europe, where he served as an international environmental and agricultural advisor. After working in sixteen countries and five war zones, his prolific writing of poetry, short stories and science resulted in many national and international publications. Wayne recently published his latest book, *Kissing the Hand of the Dead* (2013). His primary topics include Nature, the human condition, creating a new environmental ethic, and finding pragmatic ways to peace. Wayne and his wife Irina reside in San Diego. waynetwilliams@san.rr.com

Gary Winters — Gary's multicultural novel *The Deer Dancer* (2010) won awards from UC, Irvine and the San Diego Book Awards. It won Best Novel, 2010 San Diego Mensa Creative Awards; bronze 2011 Book of the Year Award for Multicultural Fiction from *ForeWord Reviews Magazine*. It is used in the curriculum at Southwestern College in the departments of Language, Literature, English, and Education. He has won awards for short story, poetry, and photojournalism. His flash fiction appears in such diverse publications as *Whisperings, University of The Virgin Islands,* and the San Diego exp/alt quarterly *Free the Marquee.* He was published in *The Guilded Pen* (2012 and 2013). Gary has been a featured reader at The Loft, UCSD; Drunk Poet's Society, Ocean Beach; Gelato Poetry Series, Old Town; and New Alchemy Poetry Series, Seaport Village. His poetry has won international awards and was published in Ireland, land of poets.

Ken Yaros, D.D.S. — Ken is an alumnus of Albright College. He received his DDS degree from Temple University. Having spent six years as a dentist with the Air Force and seven years of service with the Connecticut Air National Guard, he had the opportunity to serve in numerous locations around the world, including Vietnam. Now retired after 35 years of teaching and private practice, he has turned his hand to writing fiction and human interest stories. He was published in *The Guilded Pen* (2013) and will publish a short story on Kindle this fall.

Sandra Yeaman — Sandra spent the first 20 years of her life trying to figure out how to get away from Minnesota. She spent the next 40 years living in twelve countries, working first as a teacher, then an engineer, and finally a diplomat. She expected those exotic locations and occupations to provide her with plenty to write about, and they do. But one of the biggest surprises of her life — she often finds inspiration from her childhood and her home state. Sandra was published in *The Guilded Pen* (2013). She also blogs about her experiences and reminiscences at http://sandrayeaman.blogspot.com, her 2013 365-Project intended to develop her daily writing habit.

Amy E. Zajac — lives in San Marcos, California. Her first book, *It Started With Patton, Teresa Leska's Story, A Memoir* (2012), is her mother's compelling story as a Nazi political hostage. Amy has many stories published in anthologies since 2009, her latest is in *Chicken Soup for the Soul, From Lemons to Lemonade*, released in 2013. She was published in *The Guilded Pen* (2012 and 2013). Amy's first novel, *Foredestined*, a story of enlightenment after global destruction, was released December 2013. Currently, Amy is working on the screenplay for *Foredestined* and beginning work on a new book about roommates. E-mail: azajac10@yahoo.com.

The San Diego Writers/Editors Guild

Mission Statement: To promote, support, and encourage the writing art for adults and youth.

Founded in 1979, the Guild is believed to be the oldest writer organization in the region. The Guild is a 501(C) 3 non-profit organization. Monthly programs are planned to educate, entertain, and encourage communication among the members. A Board of Directors elected by the members directs and supports the program of work.

Benefits of membership include:
- Monthly Guild meetings
- Monthly Guild newsletter
- Periodic email newsletter
- Reduced fees for Guild-sponsored workshops
- Network with other members
- Access to critique groups
- Listing in the annual directory
- Manuscript Review Program
- Periodic presentation of awards: "The Rhoda Riddell Builders Award" — recognizing efforts to build/expand the Guild; "Special Achievements Awards" — for extraordinary service; and "The Odin Award" — to those who have been major stimulators of the writing arts in San Diego as evidenced by their body of published work.

Guild membership is open to all and guests are welcome to the meetings for a small fee. For a current list of meeting dates and speakers, go to: www.sdwritersguild.org

The Guilded Pen, Third Edition 2014
An Anthology of the San Diego Writers/Editors Guild was printed by CreateSpace, An Amazon.com Company, and is available in hard cover or e-book format at: www.CreateSpace.com/The Guilded Pen

Just write every day of your life. Read intensely. Then see what happens. Most of my friends who are put on that diet have very pleasant careers.

Ray Bradbury